Decree –
To use the P/people and creations
in such a way as to demoralize,
defile, or destroy them is an
abomination to the Lord;
Those who do so will be condemned
according to that which is written and
according to power of God against the
wrong doing of free-will,
false prophecy, and false prophesy;
Genealogy is "public information",
"Prayer Lists" are Nonsecular
"public information", Secular
Freedom of the Press is
Freedom of the Press;
Protection is in His
place, in O/our place in
which W/we dwell
and worship in the name of
Jesus Christ the Son of God,
Amen.

CONFESSIONS OF SINS
TO MAN BRINGS
CURSE,
CONFESSIONS OF SINS
TO GOD ONLY WITH
THOUGHT ONLY BRINGS
REWARD!
   (The Bible says this,
   and so I say this too.)
THERE IS NOTHING
QUEER ABOUT THE
BIBLE,
YOU MUST TRUST A
BIBLE THAT IS
CORRECT.

**You may cross reference any
book, chapter, verse, or notes with the
NKJV Study Bible
Copyright © 1997 by
"Thomas Nelson, Inc."**

**And you can translate
the Hebrew w/ the
NKJV
HEBREW-ENGLISH BIBLE
Copyright © 1996 by
"The Bible Society in Israel"**

Word

"The Basic Principle" Roman Numeral p.#xiii – interpretation
"There's only one way to interpret the Bible, but multiple ways to apply it.'

HIBD p.#[ ] – respect traditions but live by the Bible requirement

Gen. 1:26 – likeness of God requirement
"...let Us make man in Our image, according to Our likeness..."

ויאמר אלהים נעשה אדם

בצלמנו כדמותנו וירדו בדגת הים ובעוף השמים

ובבהמה ובכל-הארץ ובכל-הרמש הרמש על-

הארץ

Gen. 4:10 – blood is soul
"...the voice of your brother's blood cries out to Me from the ground."

ויאמר מה עשית קול דמי אחיך צעקים

אלי מן-האדמה

Ex. 15:26 – all healings come from the Lord prophecy Anno.

Prayer

Based on provenance.
This book is absolutely
without fabrication.
It may not be perfect;
but it came from perfection.

To my Son, Mom, & Family,
To the Church, & Young, to All
of whom I hope are Appreciative –
  This book was not so much written by
  myself as it was so much more written
  from God, His Love, and His Bible.
  This book was written for you long ago;
  This book was written for you before
  Adam and Eve were born.
  From eternity this book began.
  I carried this book before I was born.
  It has never left my mind.
  And now you know that this must have
  been written for you.
  I had to educate myself to learn how
  the Lord wanted me to communicate
  this to you.
  I wrote through 25000 papers.
  More than a hundred rough drafts.
  Edited thousands of days.
  Carried hand written for a decade.
  Had to learn the Bible; and some Hebrew.

BIBLE UNDERSTOOD:
Confess sins to God only with thought only / 1 John 5:18...

Better Version

Family "Tree of Life" John 8:51

Cover Design by HS / ADM

Copyright © 2020 Arlen D. Michaels

Published by Bible Understood:
Written by the name of Christ
All rights reserved.

ISBN: 978-0-6920-4029-4 (sc)

New King James Version Study Bible
Copyright © 1997 by Thomas Nelson Inc
Used by permission. All rights reserved.

New King James Version Hebrew-English Bible
Copyright © 1996 by The Bible Society in Israel
All rights reserved.

Holman Illustrated Bible Dictionary
Copyright © 2003 by Holman Bible Publishers.
All rights reserved.

Derek Prince Ministries(administrative ministry)
Copyright © 1998 by Peter Derek Vaughn Prince.
"They Shall Expel Demons"(Demonology)
All rights reserved.

Teach Yourself Biblical Hebrew
Copyright © 2006, 2010 Sarah Nicholson
In US: All rights reserved.

Zondervan Basics of Biblical Hebrew Grammar
Copyright © 2001 by Gary and Miles.
All rights reserved.

Teach Yourself Modern Hebrew
Copyright © 2010, 2015 Shula Gilboa
In UK: All rights reserved.

http://www.biblegateway.com

Webster's Dictionaries

Rev. date: 03/09/2021

I fought against the heat and cold from
120°F to -30 below zero.
The importance of getting this to you
was almost grave
Nearly lost my life several times before I
could–
deliver this to you!

Word

Ex. 20: 3-17 – 10 Commandments (annulled for Royal Law)

1. You shall have no other gods before Me
2. you shall not make for yourself a carved image
3. you shall not take the name of the Lord your God in vain
4. remember the Sabbath day and keep it holy
5. honor your father and mother
6. you shall not murder
7. you shall not commit adultery 'and or spiritual adultery'
8. you shall not steal
9. you shall not bear false witness against your neighbor
10. you shall not covet anything that is your neighbor's

לא

יהיה-לך אלהים אחרים על-פני לא תעשה-לך

פסל וכל-תמונה אשר בשמים ממעל ואשר

בארץ מתחת ואשר במים מתחת לארץ לא-

תשתחוה להם ולא תעבדם כי אנכי יהוה אלהיך

אל קנא פקד עון אבת על-בנים על-שלשים ועל-

רבעים לשנאי ועשה חסד לאלפים לאהבי

ולשמרי מצותי לא תשא את-שם-

יהוה אלהיך לשוא כי לא ינקה יהוה את אשר-

Ex. 20:v4 – Attachments forbidden
"...you shall not make for yourself a carved image—any likeness of anything..."

Prayer

Why this book? –
  'I am of the likeness of God,
  from whom God is "I AM",
  I am Nondenominational
  Nonsectarian Christian
  because that's what the
  Bible requires and that's
  what the Bible is; it does
  not require religion or
  denominations.
  I don't think Jesus has
  ever thought of Himself
  as a "religion" or
  "denomination",
  But the Bible was and
  is thought to Jesus by the
  Father and the Holy Spirit.
  "His word is Eternal".
  An Eternal word of God
  is "Bible",
  Bible is my vitamin drinks.
  Bible is my sugar.
  Bible is my soda pop.

Word

ישא את-שמו לשוא

זכור את-יום השבת לקדשו ששת ימים

תעבד ועשית כל-מלאכתך ויום השביעי

שבת ליהוה אלהיך לא-תעשה כל-מלאכה

אתה ובנך-ובתך עבדך ואמתך ובהמתך וגרך

אשר בשעריך כי ששת-ימים עשה יהוה את-

השמים ואת-הארץ את-הים ואת-כל-אשר-בם

וינח ביום השביעי על-כן ברך יהוה את-יום

השבת ויקדשהו כבד את-אביך

ואת-אמך למען יארכון ימיך על האדמה אשר-

יהוה אלהיך נתן לך לא תרצח

ס לא תנאף ס לא תגנב ס לא-תענה ברעך

עד שקר לא תחמד בית רעך ס

לא-תחמד אשת רעך ועבדו ואמתו ושורו וחמרו

וכל אשר לרעך

וכל-העם ראים את-הקולת ואת-הלפידם ואת

קול השפר ואת-ההר עשן וירא העם וינעו

ויעמדו מרחק ויאמרו אל-משה דבר-אתה

Prayer

Bible is my
coffee.
Bible is my
tobacco.
Bible is my
alcohol.
Bible is my
"therapist".
Bible is my
"psychologist".
Bible is my
music.
Bible is my
rest.

Bible replaces all,
I rest on "Bible".

Word

עמנו ונשמעה ואל-ידבר עמנו אלהים פן-נמות

ויאמר משה אל-העם אל-תיראו כי לבעבור

נסות אתכם בא האלהים ובעבור תהיה יראתו

על-פניכם לבלתי תחטאו

Deut. 6: 5 – the other 1 Commandment of the OT
"1. You shall love the Lord your God with all your heart, with all your soul, and with all your strength."

ואהבת את יהוה אלהיך בכל-לבבך ובכל-

נפשך ובכל-מאדך

Deut. 10:12 – fear the Lord requirement
"And now, Israel, what does the Lord your God require of you, but to fear the Lord your God..."

ועתה ישראל מה יהוה אלהיך שאל מעמך כי

אם-ליראה את-יהוה אלהיך ללכת בכל-דרכיו

ולאהבה אתו ולעבד את-יהוה אלהיך בכל-

לבבך ובכל-נפשך

Deut. 23:24 – eat from neighbor's field take none w/
"When you come into your neighbor's vineyard, you may eat your fill of grapes at your pleasure, but you shall not put any in your container."

Prayer

—Page #2 explains:
Life, salvation, and Scripture;
not death, destruction, nor reproach;
—Page #8 (How to?)- Accuracy(of
Scripture) is equally important,
—"Jesus is like a guide and the Bible
is like a map" leading us through
danger around us and why?
"Refinement" is why.
The separation of the righteous
from the wicked.
—Instructions(may I?)-
*The underlined is for thought, and
the rest is for speaking outward; except
Bible rules (conditions) for confession.*
An example of a fraction used
is as (1/6 or 2/5) means –
1 out of 6, or 2 out of 5)).
Cross References (example)-
Psalm 63 – "help from the foolish
children" *Matt. 23: 9*
Remember, prayers are
Petitions to Jesus John 14: 6
Pronunciation Key on pgs. 220, 222, &
224

—<u>Simplicity, Efficiency, Impact, and Reality,</u>
—A BOOK FOR PRAYING LESS FOR MORE (in blue) 5 MINUTES FROM 16 YEARS

Word

מוצא

שפתיך תשמר ועשית כאשר נדרת ליהוה אלהיך

נדבה אשר דברת בפיל

1 Sam. 21:13 – king David's slobber
"So he changed his behavior before them, pretended madness in their hands, scratched on the door of the gate, and let his saliva fall down on his beard."

וישם דוד את-

הדברים האלה בלבבו וירא מאד מפני אכיש

מלך-גת

1 Chr. 28: 2 – God's footstool tabernacle, earth, & enemies; almost everything [not ark or veil]

Psalm 4: 4a – be angry (w/o habit), & do not sin requirements

Psalm 4: 4b – meditate & be still requirements

Psalm 5 – "protections against spies"

Psalm 5: 1-3 – pray in the morning requirement Anno.

Psalm 10 – "protections against persecutors"

Prayer

<u>Decree</u> –
<u>To use the P/people and creations</u>
<u>in such a way as to demoralize,</u>
<u>defile, or destroy them is an</u>
<u>abomination to the Lord;</u>
<u>Those who do so will be condemned</u>
<u>according to that which is written and</u>
<u>according to power of God against the</u>
<u>wrong doing of free-will,</u>
<u>false prophecy, and false prophesy;</u>
<u>Genealogy is "public information",</u>
<u>"Prayer Lists" are Nonsecular</u>
<u>"public information", Secular</u>
<u>Freedom of the Press is</u>
<u>Freedom of the Press;</u>
<u>Protection is in His</u>
<u>place, in O/our place in</u>
<u>which W/we dwell</u>
<u>and worship in the name of</u>
<u>Jesus Christ the Son of God,</u>
<u>Amen.</u>

Word

Psalm 32: 3,5 – 1/6 Confessions of Transgressions / Anno. Rom. 4:15 "(by mouth)"

"When I kept silent, my bones grew old through my groaning all the day long."

"...I said, "I will confess my transgressions to the Lord." And You forgave the iniquity of my sin."

"Transgressions means "stepping over".

כי-החרשתי בלו עצמי

בשאגתי כל-היום

חטאתי אודיעך

ועוני לא-כסיתי

אמרתי אודה עלי פשעי ליהוה

ואתה נשאת עון חטאתי סלה

Psalm 53 – "protections against pursuers & the foolish" Matt. 23: 9

Psalm 57 – "protections against enemies"

Psalm 58 – "protections against wickedness"

Psalm 63 – "help from the foolish children" Matt. 23: 9

Prayer

Thanks – My special thanks to the people of such exquisite accuracy, simplicity, and earned reputations I look for in the sovereignty of the
— "New King James Versions" (NKJV),
— "Holman Illustrated Bible Dictionary"(HIBD),
— Peter Derek Vaughn Prince(RIP) who created "Derek Prince Ministries",
— "The Sarah Nicholson teach yourself Hebrew (Level 4)",
— The "Zondervan" company for more Biblical Hebrew,
— "The Shula Gilboa teach yourself Modern Hebrew",
— "biblegateway.com website",
— "The Webster's Dictionaries",

Word

Psalm 76 – "protections against oppressors"

Psalm 100: 4 – thanks is gate, praise is courts, (for prayer accuracy)

Psalm 104:35 – Bless the Lord, O my soul; [ ]
"...Bless the Lord, O my soul! Praise the Lord!"

יתמו חטאים מן-הארץ

ורשעים עוד אינם

ברכי נפשי את-יהוה הללו-יה

Psalm 109 – "protections against accusers"

Psalm 110 – David hears conversation God & Jesus Matt. 22:44
"...The Lord said to my Lord, "Sit at(not on) My right hand, Till I make Your enemies Your footstool..."

נאם יהוה לאדני שב לימיני

עד-אשית איביך הדם לרגליך

Psalm 112 – prayer for endurance 2 Tim. 2: 3

Psalm 116 – all men are liars in context

Prayer

    for and from those who made & make things possible not on their own accord but through Jesus, so we as People, "People" spelled w/ an uppercase "P" are truly blessed',

Our Stance – We stand before God as intercessors before men not against flesh but against demons (some spirits),

Our Foundation – Jesus,

Broad View – Using Scripture to ward off evil, &

How to? – "The Basic Principle" (Rom. numeral p.#xiii NKJVSB)- "There is only one way to interpret the Bible but multiple ways to apply it',

Location – time & Eternal overlap at least within 2 of the 3 heavens,
    This is Bible reality,
    This is my reality,
    This is your reality,

A BOOK FOR PRAYING LESS FOR MORE (in blue) 5 MINUTES FROM 16 YEARS

Endure with prayer…

Word

Psalm 127: 5 – some enemies become friends prophecy
"Happy is the man who has his quiver full of them; they shall not be ashamed, but shall speak with their enemies in the gate."

אשרי הגבר אשר מלא את-אשפתו מהם

לא-יבשו

כי-ידברו את-אויבים בשער

Psalm 147:10 – gayness forbidden 1 Cor. 6: 9-10

Prov. 4:20-22 – life(breath), & health
"My son, give attention to my words; Incline your ear to my sayings. Do not let them depart from your eyes; Keep them in the midst of your heart; For they are life to those who find them, and health to all their flesh."

בני לדברי הקשיבה

לאמרי הט-אזנך

אל-יליזו מעיניך

שמרם בתוך לבבך

כי-חיים הם למצאיהם

ולכל-בשרו מרפא

Prayer

Our Prayers Begin –
I hope, I pray, and I ask
   Holy Lord God the Father
   I ask to Jesus Christ
   the Son of God
   born from a Virgin
   if You will Hear my prayers
   don't ask me to quote this but,
   in reference to
   John 16:23,
   Holy Lord God the Father
   I ask to Jesus Christ
   the Son of God
   born from a Virgin
   if You will Hear my prayers?,
<u>I pray for my son and I ask if You
   will have mercy on him,
   help him to become
   born of God (Born Again), and
   save his soul?
   in the name of
   Jesus Christ the Son of God,
   Amen</u>
I pray Holy Lord Jesus Christ
   the Son of God
   I ask if You will
   Hear my prayers?,
I pray for "the Guide",
   the "Helper", the "Comforter",
   the Holy Spirit;

I pray for Life
    don't ask me to quote this but,
    in reference to
    John 14: 6 John 8:51 –
    Most assuredly...

Word

Eccl. 5:17 – eating in darkness forbidden
"All his days he also eats in darkness, And he has much sorrow and sickness and anger."

הנה אשר-ראיתי אני טוב אשר-

יפה לאכול-ולשתות ולראות טובה בכל-עמלו

שיעמל תחת-השתש מספר ימי-חיו אשר-נתן-

לו האלהים כי-הוא חלקו

Eccl. 7:16 – righteous in your own eyes forbidden

Isaiah 11: 2 – praising Jesus (privilege) requirement
"The Spirit of the Lord shall rest upon Him, The Spirit of wisdom and understanding, The Spirit of counsel and might, The Spirit of knowledge and of the fear of the Lord."

ונחה עליו רוח יהוה

רוח חכמה ובינה

רוח עצה וגבורה

רוח דעת ויראת יהוה

Prayer

   I say to you if anyone
   keeps My word he
   shall never see death,
   lowercase "d",
Sign of the Cross –
   in the name of the
   Father and of the Son and
   of the Holy Spirit
Prayer of Self-Exōrcism1/
   A Small List to Choose
   Against (A deliverance prayer /
   exōrcise / exōrcism)-
   the Casting out and Casting away,
   asleep and awake,
   alive or dead,
   to the bottomless pit,
   permanently, and
   I ask for Your order
   of Your approval
   Holy Lord?

Isaiah 12: 1-6 – the Exodus & reconciliation w/ water

"...O Lord, I will praise You; Though You were angry with me, Your anger is turned away, and You comfort me. Behold, God is my salvation, I will trust and not be afraid; For YAH, the Lord, is my strength. Therefore with joy you will draw water From the wells of salvation. And in that day you will say; Praise the Lord, call upon His name; Declare His deeds among the peoples, Make mention that His name is exalted. Sing to the Lord, For He has done excellent things; This is known in all the earth. Cry out and shout, [O inhabitant of Zion,] For great is the Holy One of Israel in your midst!"

Prayer

I come, I come, I come⁻
I come; I, I, I, I, I, I, I
Cast out⁻ Cast out the following
spirits, "spirits" spelled with a
lowercase "s",
the spirits of taboo,
the spirits of idols,
<u>the spirits of over-react,</u>
the spirits of pride, such as
the spirits of manipulation,
the spirits of intimidation,
the spirits of domination, and then
the spirits of violence,
the spirits of danger,
the spirits of coward,
<u>the spirits of clogged lungs,</u>
the spirits of permanent damage,
the spirits of worn-out,
<u>the spirits of arthritis,</u>
<u>the spirits of bursitis,</u>
<u>the spirits of tendinitis,</u>
<u>the spirits of schizophrenia,</u>
<u>the spirits of cancer,</u> and then
the spirits of hate, such as
the spirits of revenge, and then
the spirits of humanism,
the spirits of lust,
the spirits of reproach,

the spirits of bad-luck,
the spirits of virus,
the spirits of dehydration,
the spirits of starvation,
the spirits of hypothermia,
the spirits of heat-stroke,
the spirits of lost,

Word

ואמרת ביום ההוא

אודך יהוה כי אנפת בי

ישב אפך ותנחמני

הנה אל ישועתי

אבטח ולא אפחד

כי-עזי וזמרת יה יהוה

ויהי-לי לישועה

ושאבתם-מים בששון

ממעיני הישועה

ואמרתם ביום ההוא

הודו ליהוה קראו בשמו

הודיעו בעמים עלילתיו

הזכירו כי נשגב שמו

זמרו יהוה כי גאות עשה

מידעת זאת בכל-הארץ

צהלי ורני יושבת ציון

כי-גדול בקרבך קדוש ישראל

Prayer

    the spirits of incomplete,
    the spirits of fail,
    the spirits of unattractive,
    the spirits of poverty,
Optional –
    the spirits of
    "chronic obstructive pulmonary
    disease" which is not
    good enough for its nickname
    they call ("COPD"),
    the spirits of lung cancer,
    the spirits of collapsed lung(s),
    the spirits of lung disease,
    the spirits of emphysema,
    the spirits of pre-emphysema,
    the spirits of inflammation,
    the spirits of
    "coronary artery disease",
    the spirits of
    deteriorating esophagus,
    the spirits of cholesterol,
    the spirits of heavy chest,
    [the spirits of
    shortness of breath],

Word

Jer. 29:11 – God's thoughts toward you
"For I know the thoughts that I think toward you, says the Lord, thoughts of peace and not of evil, to give you a future and a hope."

כי אנכי ידעתי את-המחשבת

אשר אנכי חשב עליכם נאם-יהוה מחשבות

שלום ולא לרעה לתת לכם אחרית ותקוה

Hosea 4: 6 – knowledge but w/o strictness requirements
"My people are destroyed for lack of knowledge '(history)'..."

נדמו עמי מבלי הדעת

כי-אתה הדעת מאסת

ואמאסאך מכהן לי

ותשכח תורת אלהיך

אשכ חבניך גם-אני

Prayer

the spirits of asthma,
the spirits of heart disease,
the spirits of spreading disease,
the spirits of catching disease,
the spirits of hernia,
the spirits of "old",
the spirits of "muscle wasting disease",
the spirits of pestilence,
the spirits of west nile virus,
the spirits of plague,
the spirits of famine,
the spirits of "crazy eyes",
the spirits of damage,
the spirits of staph infection,
the spirits of neurosis,

Word

Joel 2:32 – use name of the Lord for Casting out
"And it shall come to pass That whomever calls on the name of the Lord Shall be saved..."

והיה כל אשר-יקרא

בשם יהוה ימלט

כי בהר-ציון ובירושלם

תהיה פליטה

כאשר אמר יהוה

ובשרידים אשר יהוה קרא

Zec. 14: 4a – Mt. Of Olives 1st & 2nd coming prophecy Anno.
"...the Messiah will return to the Mt. Of Olives '(2nd)' the very mountain from which He will have '(1st)' ascended after His time on earth..."

Zec. 14: 4b – not all will die genocide prophecy Anno. Matt. 24:22
"Christ will intervene and prevent complete genocide."

Mal. 3: 5 a – exploiting wage earners / widows / orphans forbidden

Mal. 3: 5b – turning away foreigners forbidden

Prayer

the spirits of "tooth decay",
the spirits of disproportionate,
the spirits of hesitate,
the spirits of procrastination,
the spirits of 'covet anything
that is my neighbor's,
the spirits of 'enlarged groin',
the spirits of "internal scarring",
the spirits of
"sensorineural hearing loss",
the spirits of gangrene,
the spirits of "pinched nerve",
the spirits of 'misalignment' of
my flesh and bones,
the spirits of
'talking too much',

Word

Mal. 4: 1 – fire prophecy [salvation by faith]
2 Peter 3:12

"For behold, the day is coming, Burning like an oven, And all the proud, yes, all who do wickedly will be stubble..."

כי-הנה היום בא

בער כתנור והיו כל-זדים

וכל-עשה רשעה קש

ולהט אתם היום הבא

אמר יהוה צבאות

אשר לא-יעזב להם שרש וענף

Mal. 4: 5 – Elijah then Christ prophecy
"Behold I will sent you Elijah the prophet before His coming..."

הנה אנכי שלח לכם

את אליה הנביא

לפני בוא יום יהוה

הגדול והנורא

Prayer

the spirits of
'not talking enough',
the spirits of late,
the spirits of messy,
the spirits of blasphemy (profanity),
the spirits of "the wrong
place at the wrong time",
the spirits of
low immune system,
the spirits of appendicitis,
the spirits of hardship,
the spirits of suffering,
the spirits of broken,
the spirits of
myeloproliferative disorder,
the spirits of
"planter fasciitis",
the spirits of neurotic,
the spirits of muscular-dystrophy,
the spirits of multiple-sclerosis,
the spirits of down-syndrome,
the spirits of water retention,

Word

Matt. 3: 6 – 2/6 Confessions of Sins 'John's now annulled (no longer to confess by mouth)'
"...and were baptized by him in the Jordan, confessing their sins."

והטבלו

על-ידיו בירדן כשהם מתודים על חטאתיהם

Matt. 3:11 – 4/6 Baptism in the Spirit (righteousness & judgment) Heb. 1: 7
"...He will baptize you with the Holy Spirit and fire."

אני

אמנם מטביל אתכם במים לתשובה אך הבא

אחרי חזק ממני ואינני ראוי לשאת את נעליו הוא

יטביל אתכם ברוח הקדש ובאש

Matt. 5:11 – uttering evil is forbidden
"Blessed are you when they revile and persecute you, and say all kinds of evil against you falsely for My sake."

אשריכם אם יחרפו וירדפו אתכם ויעלילו עליכם

בגללי

Matt. 5:16 – no one comes between the Christian & the Lord Anno.

Prayer

<u>the spirits of</u>
<u>hardening of the arteries,</u>
<u>the spirits of</u>
<u>"hammer-toes",</u>
<u>the spirits of allergies,</u>

Word

Matt. 5:18 – jot & tittle prophecy
"For assuredly, I say to you, till heaven and earth pass away, one jot or one tittle will by no means pass from the law till all is fulfilled."

אמן

אומר אני לכם עד אשר יעברו השמים והארץ אף

יוד אחת או תג אחד לא יעברו מן התורה בטרם

יתקים הכל

Matt. 5:20 – righteous to exceed Pharisees requirement
"For I say to you, that unless your righteousness exceeds the righteousness of the scribes and Pharisees, you will by no means enter the kingdom of heaven."

ואני אומר לכם כל

הכועס על אחיו חיב לעמד לדין האומר לאחיו

ריק חיב לעמד למשפט הסנהדרין והאומר אויל

דינו אש גיהנום

Matt. 5:22 – calling someone foolish forbidden
Matt. 23: 9

"...but whoever says, 'you fool!' shall be in danger of hell fire."

ואני אומר לכם כל

הכועס על אחיו חיב לעמד לדין האומר לאחיו

ריק חיב לעמד למשפט הסנהדרין והאומר אויל

דינו אש גיהנום

Prayer

Word

Matt. 5:34 – Jesus Forbids Oaths but… Anno.
"…any oath with God's name in it was legally binding…"

Matt. 5:37 – 'Yes' be 'Yes', 'No' be 'No' requirement
"But let your 'Yes' be 'Yes', and your 'No' 'No'…"

אך תהא מלתכם כן

כן לא לא יותר מזה מן הרע הוא

Matt. 5:41 – they say 1 mile go 2 faith requirement
"And whoever compels you to go one mile, go with him two."

ומי שמאלץ אותך ללכת אתו מרחק של מיל

אחד לך אתו שנים

Matt. 5:42 – let them use you who ask requirement
"Give to him who asks you, and from him who wants to borrow from you do not turn away."

תן למבקש ממך ואל תפנה

מן הרוצה ללוות ממך

Matt. 5:44 – pray for your enemies & persecutors
"…love your enemies…"
"…pray for those who spitefully use you and persecute you,…"

Prayer

...

Word

Matt. 6: 3 – ambidextrous & or multitasking requirement
"But when you do a charitable deed, do not let your left hand know what your right hand is doing."

ואתה בעשותך מעשה חסד אל תדע שמאלך

את אשר עושה ימינך

Matt. 6: 6 – pray & fast in secret rewards openly requirements
"...your Father who sees in secret will reward you openly."

ואתה כאשר תתפלל הכנס

לחדרך סגר את הדלת בעדך והתפלל לאביך

אשר בסתר ואביך הרואה במסתרים יגמל לך

Matt. 6: 9-13 – the Lord's Prayer

Matt. 6:15 – forgiving requirement
"But if you do not forgive men their trespasses, neither will your Father forgive your trespasses."

ואם לא תסלחו

לבני אדם גם אביכם לא יסלח לכם על

חטאתיכם

Prayer

Satan,
the Antichrist(s),
the False prophets(s),
the "principalities and powers",
Hades(the place),
Death(the place),
hades(the demon),
and
death(the demon),
from and away from myself
in the name of
Jesus Christ the Son of God,
Amen.

Word

Matt. 6:25 – worry forbidden
"Therefore I say to you, do not worry about your life, what you will eat or what you will drink; nor about your body, what you will put on..."

לכן אומר אני לכם אל תדאגו לנפשכם – מה

תאכלו או מה תשתו ולגופכם – מה תלבשו

הלא הנפש חשובה מן המזון והגוף חשוב מן

הלבוש

Matt. 7: 1 – judging forbidden
"Judge not lest ye be judged(KJV)."

אל תשפטו למען לא תשפטו

Matt. 10:19 – HS will speak for you prophecy
"...for it will be given to you in that hour what you should speak."

אבל

כאשר ימסרו אתכם אל תדאגו איך ומה תדברו

כי באותה שעה ינתן לכם מה לומר

Matt. 10:26 – all things hidden overturned
"...for there is nothing covered that will not be revealed, and hidden that will not be known."

לכן אל תפחדו מפניהם כי אין דבר מכסה

שלא יגלה ואין נסתר שלא יודע

Prayer

(or)Prayer of Self-Exōrcism2(A
 deliverance prayer / exōrcise /
 exōrcism)-
 the Casting out and Casting away,
 asleep and awake,
 alive or dead,
 to the bottomless pit,
 permanently;
 Holy Lord?,
 I Cast out a spirit,
 "spirit", spelled with a
 lowercase "s", a spirit
 called ["

"]
 from and away from myself
 in the name of
 Jesus Christ the Son of God,
 Amen.
Thanksgiving("The Gate")100: 4))-
 I thank you St. Gabriel
 the Archangel,
 I thank you St. Michael
 the Archangel,...

Word

Matt. 11:28-30 – rest from God prophecy
"Come to Me, all you who labor and are heavy laden, and I will give you rest. Take My yoke upon you and learn from Me, for I am gentle and lowly in heart, and you will find rest for your souls. For My yoke is easy and My burden is light."

בואו אלי כל העמלים

והעמוסים ואני אמציא לכם מנוחה קחו עליכם

את עלי ולמדו ממני כי ענו אני ונמוך רוח

תמצאו מרגוע לנפשותיכם כי עלי נעים וקל

משאי

Matt. 12:45 – an unclean spirit returns
"Then he goes'(in)' and takes with him seven other spirits more wicked than himself, and they enter and dwell there..."

מיד

היא הולכת ולוקחת אתה שבע רוחות אחרות

רעות ממנה וכלן נכנסות לשכן שם אכן גרועה

אחריתו של האיש ההוא מראשיתו כן גם יהיה

לדור הרע הזה

Matt. 13:24-30 – "angels will eliminate all hypocrites(unGody)" prophecy

Prayer

I thank You Holy Mary,
I thank You and I love You
Holy Lord Jesus Christ
the Son of God,
I thank You Holy Spirit,
I thank You the
Holy Lord God the Father
in the name of
Jesus Christ the Son of God,
Amen.
The Gate.

<u>Prayer of Praise1 ("God's Courtier")
100: 4))-
 Reality comes
far, far, far
from Heaven to heaven to
heaven⁻
fog at night, fog at night,
fog at night;
Snow and light, snow and light,
snow and light;
God loves quietness⁻
We are His attention
we stand before Him, ...</u>

Word

Matt. 13:45-46 – parable of the pearl
"Again, the kingdom of heaven is like a merchant seeking beautiful pearls, who, when he had found one pearl of great price, went and sold all that he had and bought it."

עוד דומה מלכות השמים לסוחר

המחפש מרגליות יפות כאשר מצא מרגלית

אחת יקרת ערך הלך ומכר את כל אשר לו וקנה

אותה

Matt. 13:57 – no honor in hometown & country prophecy
"...A prophet is not without honor except in his own country and in his own house."

" אין נביא בעירו ובביתו "

Matt. 15:11 – staying defiled forbidden
"Not what goes into the mouth defiles a man; but what comes out of the mouth..."

לא

הנכנס אל הפה מטמא את האדם אלא היוצא מן

הפה – זה מטמא את האדם

Matt. 15:20 – eat w/ washed hands not required
"...but to eat with unwashed hands does not defile a man."

אלה הם המטמאים את האדם אבל אכילה

בלא נטילת ידים אינה מטמאת את האדם

Prayer

...in honor, in honor, in honor⁻
 in honor;
 in praise, in praise, in praise⁻
 in praise;
 We pray, we pray,
 we love Him
 love never ends
 in the name of
 Jesus Christ the Son of God,
 Amen.(a song1)' /
 God's Courtier.
Prayer of Praise2("God's Courtier")-
 We are all O/one
 We are never wrong
 there is no horizon,
 We are never wrong
 there is no horizon
 We are all One,
 there is no horizon
 We are all One
 We are never wrong,
 We are all One
 We are never wrong
 there is no horizon

Prayer

in the name of
Jesus Christ the Son of God,
Amen.(a song2)' /
God's Courtier.
Prayer of Praise3("God's Courtier")-
"God Almighty
Father in Heaven who is Great,
Great in wisdom,
Great in power,
Great in His creative works,
Great in His redemptive acts,
Great in His dealings with us,
everything God is and...

Word

Matt. 16:24-25 – lose your life requirement (to deny yourself) (asceticism))

"...if anyone desires to come after Me, let him deny himself, and take up his cross, and follow Me. For whoever desires to save his life will lose it, but whoever loses his life for My sake will find it."

אז אמר ישוע לתלמידיו מי שרוצה לבוא

אחרי שיתכחש לעצמו ויקח את צלבו וילך אחרי

כי החפץ להציל את נפשו יאבד אותה אבל

המאבד את נפשו למעני ימצאנה

Matt. 17:20 – temporary faith Anno. Mark 9:49-50

"The disciples could not exōrcise the demon because they failed in faith..."

Matt. 18:19 – prayer chain

"Again I say to you that if two of you agree on earth concerning anything that they ask, it will be done for them by My Father in heaven."

עוד אומר אני לכם אם

שנים מכם יסכימו עלי אדמות בכל דבר אשר

יבקשו היה יהיה להם מאת אבי שבשמים

Matt. 19:17 – only God is Good context

Prayer

does, is
Great, Great, Great"
in the name of
Jesus Christ the Son of God,
Amen.(DPM, lost,
or unclaimed) 'a good
prayer'))
God's Courtier.
Prayer of Apologies –
  'Holy Lord?,
I apologize for sinning,
<u>getting high,</u>
<u>blaming You for my mishaps,</u>
doing the things that I have done
that I should not have done, and
for not doing the things that I
should have done called disobedience.
I [   ] am sorry
with shame(positive shame)'
in Jesus' name.

Word

Matt. 22:37, 39 – the Commandments of NT, "righteous requirement of the Law"

1. You shall love the Lord your God with all your heart, with all your soul, and with all your mind
2. you shall love your neighbors as yourself

השיב לו ישוע ואהבת את יהוה אלהיך בכל-

לבבך ובכל-נפשך ובכל מאדך

השניה דומה לה ואהבת

לרעך כמוך

Matt. 23: 9 – only One Father Matt. 5:22

"Do not call anyone on earth your father; for One is your Father, He who is in heaven."

ואל תקראו

אב לאיש מכם בארץ כי אחד הוא אביכם

שבשמים

Prayer

Prayer of Requests –
   'I hope, I pray, and I ask
Holy Lord if You will
include me in Your
Lamb's Book of Life?
If You will protect me
against the genocide,
the second death
the bottomless pit
the lake of fire called Hell,
the day which burns alike
an oven, and all dangers?
I hope, I pray, and I ask
<u>for the divine,</u> if You will help us
at all times today,
<u>divine warnings, to be liked,</u>
<u>to be healed more and faster</u>
<u>faster and more especially</u>
<u>my breathing, my knees, my neck,</u>
<u>my back,</u> my overall fitness,
health, and [   ] and
so I can help others?
I hope, I pray, and I ask
<u>for my mom's overall fitness,</u>
<u>health, and [   ]?</u>
I hope, I pray, and I ask
<u>for success for this book that You</u>
<u>helped me write?</u>

I hope, I pray, and I ask
I need much money.
<u>I hope, I pray, and I ask
for the living waters that the Bible
talks about</u> or the miracle
water people call
Deuterium Depleted water
that cures against cancer and
aging.

Word

Matt. 24:24 – claiming as false christs, false prophets forbidden

"For false christs and false prophets will rise and show great signs and wonders to deceive, if possible, even the elect."

כי יקומו

משיחי שקר ונביאי שקר ויתנו אותות גדולים

ומופתים כדי להתעות אם אפשר גם את

הבחירים

Matt. 24:27 – like lightening from east to west prophecy Anno.

"...when Christ returns, [   ] everyone will know He has arrived."

Matt. 24:36 – only God know Christ's coming Mark 13:32

"But of that day and hour no one knows, not even the angels of heaven, but My Father only."

אבל

את היום ההוא והשעה אין איש יודע גם לא

מלאכי השמים וגם לא הבן אלא האב לבדו

Prayer

I hope, I pray, and I ask
for a better than adequate
fallout shelter?
I hope, I pray, and I ask
<u>to gain thirty pounds of
mostly muscle?</u>
In the name of
Jesus Christ the Son of God,
Amen.

Confessions of Transgressions,
Sins, Faith, & Hope<u>(Heb. 10:23)</u>
<u>("The righteous requirement
of the Law brings Grace
for the
remission of sins"
Matt. 22:37, 39 Acts 2:38)</u>-
—"Confessions of
Transgressions"(sins of
known Laws)-
I confess that I had
broken the 1st, 2nd, 3rd,
4th, 5th, 7th, 8th,
maybe <u>the 9th,</u> and <u>the
10th</u> Commandments of the
OT;
<u>the other one</u> Commandment
of the OT;
<u>and the two</u> Commandments
of the NT.

OT –
1. You shall have no other gods before Me,
2. you shall not make for yourself a carved...

Word

Matt. 25:33 – separation of righteous from wicked
"And He will set His sheep on his right hand, but the goats on the left."

ויציב את הכבשים לימינו

ואת העזים לשמאלו

Matt. 27:31 – ["Stigmata"] nails in arms [not hands] Anno.

Matt. 28:19 – 2/6 Christian Baptism
"Go therefore and make disciples of all the nations, baptizing them in the name of the Father and of the Son and of the Holy Spirit..."

על כן לכו ועשו את כל

הגויים לתלמידים הטבילו אותם לשם האב והבן

ורוח הקדש

Mark 1: 4 – 1/6 John's Baptism
"John came baptizing in the wilderness and preaching a baptism of repentance for the remission of sins."

יוחנן המטביל הופיע במדבר כשהוא מכריז על

טבילה של תשובה לשם סליחת חטאים

Prayer

<u>image,</u>
<u>3. you shall not take the</u>
<u>name of the Lord your</u>
<u>God in vain,</u>
<u>4. remember the Sabbath</u>
<u>day and keep it holy,</u>
<u>5. honor your father and</u>
<u>mother,</u>

<u>7. you shall not commit</u>
<u>adultery and or spiritual adultery,</u>
<u>8. you shall not steal,</u>

<u>and maybe</u>…

<u>9. you shall not bear</u>
<u>false witness against</u>
<u>your neighbor,</u>
<u>10. you shall not covet</u>
<u>anything that is your</u>
<u>neighbor's,</u>

<u>1. You shall love the Lord</u>...

Word

Mark 9:41 – Jesus forbids religion (sectarianism)
"For whoever gives you a cup of water to drink in My name, because you belong to Christ, assuredly, I say to you, he will by no means lose his reward."

כל המשקה

אתכם כוס מים משום היתכם של המשיח אמן

אני אומר לכם שלא יאבד שכרו

Mark 9:49-50 – purifying faith Anno. Matt. 17:20
"...believers with trials that purify faith, unbelievers with the eternal fire of God's judgment."

Mark 10:45 – Christ's sacrifice (ransom / atonement)
        our sacrifice(thanksgiving, praise,
        & [works]) Psalm 116:17 Heb. 13:15
        Rom. 12: 1
"For even the Son of man did not come to be served, but to serve, and to give His life a ransom for many."

כי גם בן-האדם לא בא כדי

שישרתוהו אלא כדי לשרת ולתת את נפשו כפר

בעד רבים

Prayer

<u>your God with all your
heart, with all your soul, and
with all your strength,</u>
NT –
<u>1. You shall love the Lord
your God with all your
heart, with all your soul, and
with all your mind,
2. you shall love your
neighbor as yourself,</u>
confessions of transgressions
in the name of
Jesus Christ the Son of God,
Amen.
—"Confessions of Sins" –
<u>I confess that I had sinfully
worshiped Satan indirect-
ly,</u>

<u>I confess that I had and had used
"Outbursts of Wrath",</u>

Word

Mark 12:17 – give to Caesar(material), give to God(P/people)
"...render to Caesar the things that are Caesar's and to God the things that are God's..."

אמר להם ישוע את

אשר לקיסר תנו לקיסר ואת אשר לאלהים –

לאלהים הם השתוממו עליו

Mark 16:17 – casting out demons(ekballo) prophecy DPM p.#16 ADM
"And these signs will follow those who believe: In My name they will cast out demons; they will speak with new tongues;

"Been subject to demonic influence'

'Being possessed by the devil(or, not and)'

Luke 6:27 – Love your enemies requirement
"But I say to you hear: Love your enemies, do good to those who hate you, bless those who spitefully use you."

אבל אליכם השומעים אומר אני אהבו את

אויביכם היטיבו עם שונאיכם

Prayer

I confess that before I
was in my mother's womb
I had been possessed
by demons accumulated
from the past four
generations(Ex. 20: 5)
womb to womb
alike most P/people,

<u>I confess that I had
and had used Pride,</u>

<u>I confess that I had
and had used Lust,</u>

<u>I confess that I had
hurt some animals,</u>

<u>[I confess three confessions
I leave unwritten for
respect to four persons],</u>

I confess that I had
hurt my own body of
flesh and bones
through-out my life
<u>mostly with toxins,</u>

<u>I confess that I had
been mischievous toward most
P/people I've been
associated with,</u>

Luke 6:29a – turn the other cheek requirement

"To him who strikes you on one cheek, offer the other also..."

המכה

אותך על הלחי הטה לו גם את השניה הלוקח

את מעילך אל תמנע ממנו גם את כתנתך

Luke 6:29b – give to he who steals requirement
Luke 6:27

"...and from him who takes away your cloak, do not withhold your tunic either."

המכה

אותך על הלחי הטה לו גם את השניה הלוקח

את מעילך אל תמנע ממנו גם את כתנתך

Luke 9:62 – looking back from doing God's will forbidden

"...no one, having put his hand to the plow, and looking back, is fit for the kingdom of God."

השיב לו ישוע מי ששם את ידו על המחרשה

ומביט אחורנית לא יכשר למלכות האלהים

Prayer

"I confess I cannot
walk in Holiness by my
own power or strength",

I confess I have
"positive shame" <u>(HIBD said req.</u>),

I confess I [have] or
[had] missed communion
<u>this month,</u>
confessions of sins
in the name of
Jesus Christ the Son of God,
Amen
—"Confession of Belief"
also known as—
—"Confession of Faith" –
I confess Jesus is Lord
and in my heart
I believe that Christ
was raised from the
dead
confession of faith
in the name of
Jesus Christ the Son of God,
Amen
—"Confession of Hope" –
I confess that I have hope
<u>("for rest")</u>
confession of hope
in the name of
Jesus Christ the Son of God,
Amen

Word

Luke 12:48 – much given, much required
"...for everyone to whom much is given, from him much is required..."

אבל זה שלא ידע

ועשה דברים שהוא חיב עליהם מכות יכה מעט

כל מי שנתן לו הרבה ידרש ממנו הרבה ומי

שהפקד בידו הרבה ידרשו ממנו עוד יותר

Luke 12:50 – 3/6 Baptism of Suffering
"But I have a baptism to be baptized with, and how distressed I am till it is accomplished!"

אלא שעלי להטבל טבילה ומה

כבדה עלי המועקה עד אשר תשלם

Luke 21:36 – watch, stay awake(figuratively), & pray requirements Matt. 26:38
"Watch therefore and pray always that you may be counted worthy to escape'& exōrcise' all these things that will come to pass, and to stand before the Son of Man."

לכן עמדו על

המשמר בכל עת והתפללו שיהיה בכחכם להמלט

מכל העמידות האלה ולהתיצב לפני בן-האדם

Prayer

I hope, I pray, and I ask
   for my immediate family for
   "Life, Breath, and Health"
   in reference to
   Prov. 4:20-22 –
   Give attention to my words;
   Incline your ear
   to my sayings.
   Do not let them depart
   from your eyes;
   Keep them in the midst
   of your heart;
   For they are life to
   those who find them,
   And health to all their
   flesh
   in the name of
   Jesus Christ the Son of God,
   Amen.
I hope, I pray, and I ask
   for ["

                                     "]

   for "Life, Breath, and Health"
   in reference to
   Prov. 4:20-22 – ...

Word

Luke 22:19 – Communion requirement (or confession to God)
"...this is My body which is given for you; do this in remembrance of Me."

לקח את הלחם ברך ובצע ונתן להם

באמרו זה גופי הנתן בעדכם זאת עשו לזכרי

John 1:14 – Jesus is God & Man Anno.
"And the word became flesh and dwelt among us, and we beheld His glory, the glory as of the only begotten of the Father, full of grace and truth."

"...God became human..."

הדבר נהיה בשר ושכן בתוכנו ואנחנו ראינו את

כבודו כבוד בן יחיד מלפני אביו מלא חסד ואמת

John 1:17 – grace by Royal Law Eph. 2: 8-9
"For the law was given through Moses, but grace and truth came through Jesus Christ."

כי התורה נתנה על-ידי משה והחסד

והאמת באו דרך ישוע המשיח

Prayer

Give attention to my words; Incline your ear to my sayings.
Do not let them depart from your eyes;
Keep them in the midst of your heart;
For they are life to those who find them,
And health to all their flesh
in the name of
Jesus Christ the Son of God,
Amen

I pray for Protections against all persecutions & all persecutors(Ps. #10)-

Why do You stand afar off, O Lord? Why do You hide in times of trouble? The wicked in his pride persecutes the poor; let them be caught in the plots which they have devised. For the wicked boasts of his heart's desire; he blesses the greedy and renounces the Lord. The wicked in his proud countenance does not seek God;

God is in none of his thoughts.
His '(his)' ways are always
prospering; Your judgments
are far above, out of sight;
as for all his enemies,
he sneers at them.
He has said in his heart, "I shall not

Word

John 3:18 – "atmosphere of reward" / nonbelievers condemned already

"He who believes in Him is not condemned; but he who does not believe is condemned already…"

המאמין בו איננו נדון מי שאיננו מאמין

כבר נדון מפני שלא האמין בשם בן-האלהים

היחיד

John 5:28 – resurrection; trumpet… (corruption & or immortality) prophecy
1 Cor. 15:52-53

"Do not marvel at this; for the hour is coming in which all who are in graves will hear His voice."

אל תתמהו על זאת

כי תבוא שעה שכל שוכני קבר ישמעו את קולו

John 8:51 – Eternal Life

"Most assuredly, I say to you, if anyone keeps My word he shall never see death."

אמן אמן אני

אומר לכם אם ישמר איש את דברי לא יראה מות

לעולם

Prayer

be moved; I shall never
be in adversity." His
mouth is full of cursing
and deceit and oppression;
under his tongue is trouble
and iniquity. He sits in
the lurking places of the
villages; in the secret
places he murders the
innocent; his eyes are
secretly fixed on the helpless.
He lies in wait secretly, as a lion
in his den; He lies in wait to catch
the poor; He catches the poor
when he draws him into his net.
So he crouches, he lies low,
That the helpless may fall by his
strength. He has said in his heart,
"God has forgotten;
He hides His face;
He will never see."
Arise, O Lord!
O God, lift up Your hand!
Do not forget the humble.
Why do the wicked renounce God?
He has said in his heart,
"You will not require an account."
But You have seen, for You observe

trouble and grief,
To repay it by Your hand.
The helpless commits himself to You;
You are the helper of the fatherless.
Break the arm of the wicked and
the evil man; seek out his
wickedness until You find

Word

John 12:25 – hate your life requirement (deny yourself) Matt. 16:24

"He who loves his life will lose it, and he who hates his life 'altar' in this world will keep it for eternal life."

האוהב את נפשו

מאבד אותה והשונא את נפשו בעולם הזה

ישמרנה לחיי עולם

John 14: 6 – pray to Jesus by petition requirement Psalm 100: 4

"...no one comes to the Father except through Me."

אמר לו ישוע אני הדרך והאמת והחיים אין

איש בא אל האב אלא דרכי

John 14:23 – love for God & His word requirement

"Jesus answered and said to him, "If anyone loves Me, he will keep My word, and My Father will love him, and We will come to him and make Our home with him."

השיב לו ישוע מי שאוהב אותי ישמר את

דברי ואבי יאהב אותו גם נבוא אליו ונשכן אצלו

John 15:18 – The "World's" Hatred
"If the world hates you, you know that it hated Me before it hated you."

אם העולם שונא אתכם דעו כי אותי שנא

ראשונה

Prayer

none. The Lord is King
forever and ever; the
nations have perished out
of His land. Lord, You
have heard the desire
of the humble; You will
prepare their heart; You
will cause Your ear to
hear, To do justice to
the fatherless and the
oppressed, that the man
of the earth may oppress
no more
in the name of
Jesus Christ the Son of God,
Amen.

Word

John 16: 2 – apostles rejected; prophecy

**John 16: 8 – sin, righteousness, & judgment
"(concerns of a true Church)"**
"And when He has come, He will convict(not convince) the world of sin, and of righteousness, and of judgment."

כאשר יבוא יוכיח את

העולם על חטא ועל צדק ועל משפט

John 17:21 – (all may be one) / Anno. / not by Church but by love 13:35 / 1 Cor. 12:27-28a
"...this is what Jesus was commanding in 13:34, 35..."

"...by this all will know that you are My disciples, if you have love for one another."

בזאת ידעו

הכל שתלמידי אתם אם תהיה אהבה ביניכם

Prayer

I recite the sixty-six books of the (NKJV) '<u>a bible that cares</u>' –
OT –
   Gen.
   Ex.
   Lev.
   Num.
   Deut.
   Josh.
   Ruth
   1 Sam.
   2 Sam.
   1 Kin.
   2 Kin.
   1 Chr.
   2 Chr.
   Ezra
   Neh.(Nē hi mī āh)
   Esth.(Ěs těr)
   Job
   Ps.
   Prov.
   Eccl.
   Song(of Solomon)
   Is.
   Jer.

Lam.[   ]
Ezek.
Dan.
Hos.(Hō zay^a)
Joel
Amos(Aymōs)
Obad.
Jon.

Word

John 18:37 – w/ truth comes voice; prophecy
"...everyone who is of the truth hears My voice."

אמר לו פילטוס אם כן אתה מלך ענה

ישוע אתה אומר שאני מלך לכך אני נולדתי

ולשם כך באתי לעולם כדי שאעיד על האמת כל

אשר הוא מן האמת שומע לקולי

John 19:11 – God decides events

Acts 2: 1-4 – Bible evidence of tongues on Pentecost

Acts 2:38a – 4/6 Baptism in the Spirit ["Confirmation"] by Spirit [& water]
"...repent, and let every one of you be baptized in the name of Jesus Christ for the remission of sins; and you shall receive the gift of the Holy Spirit."

אמר להם כיפא שובו בתשובה והטבלו איש

איש מכם בשם ישוע המשיח לסליחת חטאיכם

ותקבלו את מתנת רוח הקדש

Acts 2:38b – repentance (remission of sins)

Prayer

Mic.(Mī cāh)
Nah.(Nayhᵃm)
Hab.(Hᵃ băk kᵃk)
Zeph.
Hag.(Hăg gī)
Zech.
Mal.
NT –
   Matt.
   Mark
   Luke
   John
   Acts
   Rom.
   1 Cor,
   2 Cor.
   Gal.
   Eph.(Ē phē shěnz)
   Phil.
   Col.
   1 Thess.
   2 Thess.
   1 Tim.
   2 Tim.
   Titus
   Philem.(Phī lē mŏn)
   Heb.
   James

1 Pet.
2 Pet.
1 John
2 John
3 John
Jude
Rev.

Word

Acts 6: 2b – force to work forbidden
"It is not desirable that we should leave the word of God and serve tables."

קראו שנים-עשר השליחים את המון

התלמידים ואמרו לא רצוי שאנחנו נעזב את דבר

אלהים ונשרת בשלחנות

Acts 15:39 – Christians will not agree on everything
       Anno. Acts 21:25

Acts 17:32 – the flesh(body) is not evil Anno.

Acts 21: 8 – Philip the Evangelist
      [Matt. Mark Luke John]

Acts 21:25 – we honor the same Lord
       Anno. 2 Cor. 11: 4 Acts 15:39

Prayer

I hope, I pray, and I ask
   Holy Lord Jesus Christ
   the Son of God; will You
   ask the Holy Lord God the
   Father only those who do not
   trouble me for Christians do not
   trouble, if He will give belief
   to all unbelievers,
   if He will teach many
   people self-exōrcism,
   if He will save and provide
   for all or any of His
   believers, Christians, and creations
   to be mentioned and not mentioned
(The 6 Armors) –
   The six armors which is the
   girdle of truth,
   breastplate of righteousness,
   sandals of gospel,
   shield of faith,
   helmet of salvation,
   sword of the Spirit;

(The 9 Gifts) –
   The nine gifts which is
   wisdom, knowledge, faith, healings,
   miracles, prophecy,
   discernings of S/spirits,
   kinds of tongues,
   interpretations of tongues;
(The 9 Fruits) –
   The nine fruits which is
   love, joy, peace, longsuffering,
   kindness, goodness, faithfulness,
   gentleness, self-control...

Word

Rom. 2:11 – "no one is partial to judgment"
James 2: 8-9
"For there is no partiality with God."

כי אין

משוא פנים עם האלהים

Rom. 6:14 – not under L/law but under grace
"For sin shall not have dominion over you, for you are not under law but under grace."

החטא לא ישלט בכם כי אינכם תחת

יד התורה אלא תחת יד החסד

Rom. 8:15 – adopted by the Spirit
"For you did not receive the spirit of bondage again to fear, but you received the Spirit of adoption by whom we cry out "Abba, Father."

הרי לא קבלתם רוח של עבדות

לחזר אל הפחד אלא קבלתם רוח המקנה מעמד

של בנים וברוח זאת אנו קוראים אבא אבינו

Rom. 8:18 – glory of God for man also
"For I consider that the sufferings of this present time are not worthy to be compared with the glory which shall be revealed in us."

אני סבור שסבלות הזמן הזה אינם שקולים

כנגד הכבוד העתיד להגלות בנו

Prayer

<u>(The 8 Church Qualities)</u> –
   The eight church qualities which is
   apostles, prophets, teachers, miracles,
   healings, helps, administrations, tongues;
<u>"Triune Being"</u> –
I pray if we may be in His hands
   our spirits,
   our souls, and
   our bodies?,
<u>Restoration</u> –
   for the restoration of
   our spirits,
   our souls, and
   our bodies who qualify?,
<u>Repentance</u> –
   for or from
   true repentance?,
<u>Ransom("Bought w/ Blood")</u> –
   from the atoning death of
   Jesus Christ upon the Cross,

Word

Rom. 10: 9 – 5/6 Confession of Faith "(by mouth)"
"That if you confess with your mouth the Lord Jesus and believe in your heart that God has raised Him from the dead, you will be saved."

ואם אתה מודה

בפיך שישוע הוא האדון ומאמין בלבבך שאלהים

הקים אותו מן המתים – תושע

Rom. 10:10 – righteousness & salvation requirements

Rom. 10:17 – w/ faith comes hearing prophecy
"So then faith comes by hearing, and hearing by the word of God."

לפיכך האמונה באה

בשמיעה והשמיעה – בהכרזת דבר המשיח

Rom. 12:15 – weep w/ those who weep requirement
"Rejoice with those who rejoice, and weep with those who weep."

שמחו עם השמחים

ובכו עם הבוכים

Rom. 12:16 – wise in your opinion forbidden

Rom. 12:17 – evil to evil forbidden

Prayer

(<u>Priesthood, kingship,
Humanity, and History
(HIBD</u>))-
I pray according to
  Priesthood, kingship,
  Humanity, and History;
(<u>Prayer List</u>) –
I pray for and from Adam to
  Abraham, for and from
  Abraham to Issac,
  [Jacob 1],
  Judāh,
  Pērĕz,
  Zērāh,
  Tamar(Taymār),
  Hĕzrŏn,
  Ram,
  Amminadab(^{a}mmin^{a}dăb),
  Năshŏn,
  Sălmŏn,
  Bōăz,

Word

Rom. 13 – to resist authority brings judgment on oneself Anno. James 1:20 (trials, anger, & w/o glory)

"...trying to understand the other person's position, leaving the rest to God.'

1 Cor. 2: 4b, 5 – "*human wisdom" is the demon humanism forbidden; Col. 2: 8 p.#P

"...*human wisdom,* but in the demonstration of the Spirit and of power,"

"that your faith should *not be in the wisdom of men* but in the power of God."

1 Cor. 3:16-17a – my flesh is God's flesh

"Do you not know that you are the temple of God and that the Spirit of God dwells in you? If anyone defiles the temple of God, God will destroy him..."

האם אינכם יודעים כי היכל אלהים אתם וכי

רוח אלהים שוכנת בקרבכם אם ישחית איש

את היכל אלהים אלהים ישחית אותו כי היכל

האלהים קדוש ואתם היכלו

1 Cor. 6 – Do not Sue the Brethren requirement Anno. / Obadiah Commentary

"...making a mockery of Christians by feuding in public."

Prayer

Rayhăb,
Ōběd,
Ruth,
Jesse,
king David,
Solomon,
Rehoboam(Rēhŏbō^am),
Abijah(^abījă),
Asa(Ăss^a),
Jehoshaphat(Jihŏsh^aphăt),
Joram(Jōr^am),
Uzziah(^azzī^a),
Jotham(Jōth^am),
Ahaz(Ayhăz),
Hezekiah(Hězěkī^ah),
Manasseh(M^anăs^a),
Amon(Aymŏn),
Josiah(Jōsī^a),
Jechoniah(Jěchōnī^a),
Shealtiel(Shi ăl tiěl),
Zerubbabel(Zě r^ab b^a běl),
Abiud(Ābī^ad),

Word

1 Cor. 6: 9-10 – forbidden
"...neither fornicators, nor idolaters, nor adulterers, nor homosexuals, nor sodomites, nor thieves, nor covetous, nor drunkards, nor revilers, nor extortioners will inherit the kingdom of God."

או שמא

אינכם יודעים כי עושי עול לא יירשו את מלכות

האלהים אל תטעו לא זונים ולא עובדי אלילים

לא מנאפים ולא עושי זמה ולא יודעי משכב זכר

לא גנבים ולא חמדנים לא סובאים ולא מגדפים

ולא חומסים יירשו את מלכות האלהים

1 Cor. 10: 1-4 – Jesus' Spirit was involved in the Exodus

1 Cor. 11: 4 – men do not cover head in prayer requirement

1 Cor. 11: 5 – women cover head in prayer requirement

1 Cor. 11: 7, 14 – long hair on men forbidden

1 Cor. 12: 8-10 – the nine gifts

1 Cor. 12:13 – the Spirit surrounded us before Christ;
              & indwells us since Christ Anno.

Prayer

Eliakim(Ēlīᵃkim),
Azor(Ayzŏr),
Zadok(Zaydŏk),
Achim(Aykim),
Eliud(Ilīᵃd),
Eleazar(Ěl i ay zᵃr),
Matthan(Mǎt thǎn),
[Jacob2],
Joseph,
Mary,
Intercessors – Jesus Christ,
and myself(Christian requirement),
Immediate family – my mom, <u>my sister,</u>
my dad(<u>s</u>), <u>my son,</u>
<u>my niece, my nephew,</u>
my grandmas, my grandpas,
<u>my aunts, my uncles,</u>
<u>my cousins, my brother-in-law,</u>
infants,
babies,
children,
teenagers,
A Category of its own – ...

Word

1 Cor. 12:27-28a – People are Churches, & Churches are Churches EQUALLY Rev. 21:22 Anno. / John 17:21

"Now you'(temples)' are the body of Christ, and members individually." "And God has appointed these'(churches)' in the church: first apostles,..."

"People, Christ, and Church are temples'

אתם גוף המשיח ואיבריו איש איש לפי חלקו

ומהם הקים אלהים בקהלה – ראשית שליחים

שנית נביאים שלישית מורים אחרי כן עושי נסים

אחרי כן מתנות הרפוי עזרה לזולת הנהגה ומיני

לשונות

1 Cor. 12:28b – 8 Church qualities

"And God has'(not everyday)' appointed these in the church: first apostles, second prophets, third teachers, after that miracles, then gifts of healings, helps, administrations, varieties of tongues."

ומהם הקים אלהים בקהלה – ראשית שליחים

שנית נביאים שלישית מורים אחרי כן עושי נסים

אחרי כן מתנות הרפוי עזרה לזולת הנהגה ומיני

לשונות

Prayer

to free and prevent all
victims of flesh and bones from
all prisons against all brutalities and
the spirits of negligence
from Satan of
men's judgments Matt. 7: 1
"All or any of the persecuted
Christian Churches through-out
the world especially within
Iraq and Syria",
Peter Derek Vaughn Prince,
Derek Prince Ministries(maybe w/
Dick Leggatt, Gina, Nan, Janice, Terry,
Christine, [   ], Less,
Charlotte, Nicole, [   ],
Allen, Norma, Juanita,
Terri, John, Jenny, Brad, Mike),
"the Garland Church",
"our political leaders",
war veterans "and their families",
"my local city(town)"
(Mark 9:38-41),
Celebrities – Cain, Judas Iscariot, and then
a specific P/person who had
depression and stuff [   ],
Charles Manson,
Jeffrey Dahmer,
Adolf Hitler,

Michael Jackson,
Burt Reynolds, John Candy,
Christopher Reeve,
Nick Nolte, Richard Pryor,
Anna Nicole Smith,
Marilyn Monroe,
Whitney Houston, Mel Gibson,
Johnny Cash,

Word

1 Cor. 13: 8 – Love Overrides; prophecies, tongues, & knowledge

1 Cor. 14:40 – decency & order requirements

1 Cor. 15:57 – "thanks through Jesus is our victory"
John 14: 6
"But thanks be to God, who gives us the victory through our Lord Jesus Christ."

אבל תודה לאלהים הנותן לנו

את הנצחון על-ידי אדוננו ישוע המשיח

2 Cor. 2:17 – peddling[panhandling] for prophet forbidden

2 Cor. 5: 1 – life isn't what it seems
"For we know that if our earthly house, this tent, is destroyed, we have a building from God, a house not made with hands, eternal is the heavens."

אנו יודעים שאם יהרס בית משכננו הארצי יש

לנו בנין מאת אלהים בית שאינו מעשה ידים והוא

בשמים לעולמים

2 Cor. 9: 8 – want restriction Anno.
"...God sees to it that the generous giver will not suffer want..."

Prayer

Elvis, Kris Kristofferson,
Sam Kinison, Ice-Cube,
Evel Knievel, Robert Downing Jr.,
Cassius Marcellus Clay Jr.,
Martha Stewart, Snoop Dogg,
Justin Bieber, Michael Douglas,
Kathleen Turner, Nikola Tesla,
Jackie Onassis,
Arnold Schwarzenegger,
Geraldo Rivera,
St. Anthony1 the Great(Egypt),
St. Francis of Assisi,
a man named Crazy Horse,
Ozzy Osbourne,
Charlton Heston,
Stephen [Hawking],
Neil Young, Merle Haggard,
Willy Nelson,
Henry Fonda, Peter Fonda,
Jane Fonda, Ted Turner,
Robert Redford,
Frank W. Dux,
Ip Man,
John McCain,
Roger McGuinn,
Michael J. Fox,
Christopher Lloyd,
Molly Ringwald,

Kurt Russell,
Dennis Rodman,
Randy Quaid, Dennis Quaid,
John Merrik, Al Pacino,
Randy Cramer, Corey Goode,
Cherilyn Sarkisian, Sean Hannity,
Alex Trebek,
a man called [Onslow],
Don King,
Carol Kane,
Michael Johnathon,

Word

2 Cor. 10: 8 – words that *tear down* forbidden [Anno.]

"For even if I should boast somewhat more about our authority, which the Lord gave us for edification and not for your *destruction*, I shall not be ashamed..."

וגם אם אתגאה קצת יותר מדי

בסמכות אשר נתן לנו האדון לבנות ולא להרס

לא אבוש

2 Cor. 11: 4 – preaching another Jesus or another gospel forbidden Anno. Acts 21:25

"For if he who comes preaching another Jesus whom we have not preached, or if you receive a different spirit which you have not received, or a different gospel which you have not expected—you may well put up with it!"

"...fear and bondage vs faith and freedom.'

שכן

אם בא מישהו ומכריז לכם על ישוע אחר אשר לא

הכרזנו או בקבלכם רוח שונה מזו שנתנה לכם

או בשורה שונה מזו שקבלתם אזי אתם סובלים

אותו היטב

2 Cor. 12: 2 – the 3 H/heavens Anno.
"it was common to speak of three heavens"

Prayer

My Biological Family,
My Christian Family,
and Others –
    All the others of the
    following of my biological family,
    <u>Margaret and family,</u>
    my Christian family,
    <u>Krista's brother and Krista and</u>
    <u>the others of her family by request,</u>
    <u>David / Deborah / Aaron / Priscilla /</u>
    <u>Sheila / and David junior Holmes,</u>
    <u>grandma Monica and grandpa Louis,</u>
    <u>grandma Fern and grandpa Howard,</u>
    <u>grandma Betty and grandpa Tiny,</u>
    <u>Glenn, Little Alan,</u>
    <u>Aimee Daigh(nickname "Bear"),</u>
    <u>Rab, Kirby,</u>
    <u>Pam Kanis, Pearl, Frank,</u>
    <u>Jean and Al,</u>
    <u>Brian(Shane's friend),</u>
    <u>Kena,</u>
    <u>Brad and his family from "Maverik",</u>
    <u>Nina Tomasewski,</u>
    <u>Gerald Spiker,</u>

Josh McLean and his family
by request,
Doug, [Misti], John, Kenny,
Bill Lye, Gus, Oscer,
[Margaret] Scranton,

Word

Gal. 5:19-21 – forbidden
"Now the works of the ' flesh are evident, which are: adultery, fornication, uncleanness'(w/o purity)', lewdness, idolatry, sorcery'(witchcraft)', *hatred, contentions, jealousies, outbursts of wrath, selfish ambitions, dissensions, heresies, envy, murders, drunkenness, revelries, and the like..."

מעשי הבשר גלויים

ואלה הם נאוף וזנות טמאה זמה עבודת

אלילים כשוף שנאה מדון צרות עין כעס

מריבה מחלוקות כתות קנאה שכרות

הוללות וכדומה אומר אני לכם מראש מה

שכבר אמרתי עושי מעשים כאלה לא יירשו את

מלכות האלהים

Gal. 5:22-23 – the 9 fruits

Gal. 5:24 – "1 of 2 marks1 of a true believer / Christian" 2 Tim. 2:19 p.#M
"And those who are Christ's have crucified the flesh with its passions and desires."

האנשים השיכים למשיח צלבו את בשרם

עם תשוקותיו ותאוותיו

Prayer

Donny and Artel,
Aunt Mac, Kathryn, [Tilly],
Patty and Leroy, Gaylene,
Uncle Leroy, Jim Farns,
Diane and Fran,
Darlene her mom and Steve,
Ed and Alice,
Amelinda and Kevin Olsen,
Val and Jerry,
Bridget and her children,
Tony, Caleb,
Rani / Henry Otis / Matthew and
Matthew's mom,
Deloris White,
Shana Hutzenbiler,
Merle and Shirley Lange,
John and Anne Parker,
Heather(Little Alan's girlfriend),
Leroy and Andrea Hutzenbiler,
Chris Petroff,

Word

Eph. 2: 8-9 – grace only from faith; faith requirement John 1:17

"For by grace you have been saved through faith, and that not of yourselves; it is the gift of God, not of works, lest anyone should boast."

הן

בחסד נושעתם על-ידי האמונה וזאת לא מידכם

כי אם מתנת אלהים היא אין זה נובע ממעשים

כדי שלא יתגאה איש

Eph. 6:12 – war against demons not flesh requirement

"For we do not wrestle against flesh and blood, but against principalities, against powers, against the rulers of darkness of this age, against spiritual hosts of wickedness in the heavenly places."

כי לא עם בשר-ודם מלחמה לנו

אלא עם רשיות ושררות עם מושלי חשכת העולם

הזה עם כחות רוחניים רעים בשמים

Eph. 6:13-17 – the 6 armors

Prayer

<u>Big Alan and Shannon,</u>
<u>Johnny and Betty Jo McCoy,</u>
<u>Hubert and [Jessi],</u>
<u>John O'Malley,</u>
<u>Scott McWilliams,</u>
<u>Dick and Dotsy,</u>
<u>Gary and Mareen, [Gaga](gāgā),</u>
<u>Heidi and her children,</u>
<u>Kelly, Tina, Dan,</u>
<u>Gerald and Reetha Baehm,</u>
<u>Jack and Connie Godak,</u>
<u>Floyd and Betty Hutzenbiler,</u>
<u>Bob and Karla Rankin,</u>
<u>Jim Smart,</u>
<u>George and Mary Althoff,</u>
<u>Carl and Jan Christman,</u>
<u>Bob and Carol Greenwood,</u>
<u>Jim and Mary Anne Staudingger,</u>
<u>Nancy Sanchez,</u>
<u>Don and Cindy Buechler,</u>
<u>Clarence and Kate Berry,</u>

Word

Phil. 2:10 – genuflect at the word of Christ requirement
"...that at the name of Jesus every knee should bow, of those in heaven, and of those on earth, and of those under the earth."

למען תכרע

בשם ישוע כל ברך בשמים ובארץ ומתחת לארץ

Col. 2: 8 – humanism; philosophy... prophecy forbidden DPM p.#84 p.#P 1 Cor. 2: 4b, 5
"Beware lest anyone cheat you through philosophy and empty deceit..."

"...humanism has its roots in Greek philosophy... the way for the rise of the Antichrist."

הזהרו שאיש לא יוליך אתכם שולל

בפילוסופיה ובתעתועי הבל על-פי מסורות של

בני אדם על-פי עקרי העולם ולא על-פי המשיח

Prayer

Ron and Rosa [Devier],
Richard and Clare Hutzenbiler,
Phil and Judy Parker,
Ken and Cheryl Anne Syndergaard,
Kenneth and Holly Buech,
Kerry Parker, [Tom],
Vonda and her husband,
Bob('Doughboy')compliment)),
James, Mike Chambers,
Tim,
Rebecka / her youngest daughter /
her yougest son / Robby and Corbin,
Victor, Dan, [Damian],
Joe Sandavol, Danial,
Josh, Mike, Mitch, Fred,
Troy, Danial Cordova, Bo,
Leroy, Donna, Bob Hart,
Clint,
Bob nickname "Forkhorse",

Word

Col. 2:20 – strictness(denominations) forbidden
"Therefore, if you died with Christ from the basic principles of the world, why, as though living in the world, do you subject yourselves to regulations."

אם מתם עם המשיח לגבי עקרי העולם למה

אתם נוהגים כמו אנשים החיים בעולם ונכנעים

לחקים

1 Thess. 5: 3 – God decides peace and safety (not men) prophecy
"For when they say, "Peace and safety!" then sudden destruction comes upon them, as labor pains upon a pregnant woman..."

כאשר יאמרו הבריות שלום

ובטחון אז יבוא עליהם שבר פתאום כצירי לדה

על אשה הרה ולא יוכלו להמלט

1 Thess. 5:23 – the Triune Being
(not the Asian version)

"...and may your whole spirit, soul, and body be preserved blameless at the coming of our Lord Jesus Christ."

יקדש אתכם אלהי השלום קדשה שלמה

ותשמר שלמות רוחכם ונפשכם וגופכם להיות

בלי דפי בבוא אדוננו ישוע המשיח

Prayer

<u>Jack nickname "Big Jack",</u>
<u>Jack nickname "Little Jack",</u>
<u>Larry Oster,</u>
<u>Victor the chef,</u>
<u>Sammy Swartze and</u>
<u>Betty Johnson,</u>
<u>Eric,</u>
<u>Ron and Earl,</u>
<u>guy who either called or</u>
<u>calls himself "Cotton",</u>
<u>Robin Flowers, Cedric,</u>
<u>Jim, Matt Tuey, Theodora,</u>
<u>Randy Propp,</u>
<u>Roxanne and a guy who</u>
<u>either called or calls him-</u>
<u>self "Tennessee",</u>
<u>Terry who either called or</u>
<u>calls himself "the carpet layer",</u>
<u>Kelli, Lorna Flack and Jessy,</u>
<u>Darla, Peggy Lasiter,</u>
<u>Myron and Milly,</u>

Word

2 Thess. 1: 7 – When Jesus comes so will rest prophecy
"...and to give you who are troubled rest with us when the Lord Jesus is revealed from heaven with His mighty angels..."

ולתת לכם הנרדפים רוחה יחד עמנו כאשר

יתגלה האדון ישוע מן השמים עם מלאכי עזו

1 Tim. 6:20-21 – idle talk forbidden 2 Tim. 2:14
"...avoid the profane and idle babblings and contradictions of what is falsely called knowledge—by professing it some have strayed concerning the faith..."

טימותיאוס שמר את הפקדון סור מדבורים

תפלים וחסרי קדשה ומטענות ופרכות של מה

שבכזב מכנה דעת יש שהתימרו בה וסטו מן

האמונה החסד עמכם אמן

2 Tim. 2: 3 – perseverance(endurance) requirement
"You therefore must endure hardship as a good soldier of Jesus Christ."

השתתף בסבל כחיל טוב של

המשיח ישוע

Prayer

James Hanson,
Cathy / Billy Jo Borring,
Charlie, Trevor,
Rich, Cole, Marlena,
Jerry Cox, Cody, Roger,
and the other Rodger either
called or calls himself
"Rodger Dodger",
Terry either called or calls
himself "T-Bone",
a couple of male twins
nicknamed "the twins",
Chris Badwound,
guy who either called or
calls himself "Shoes",
Shandy / Jack,
Vicky, Vivian, Tracy,
Steve Miller, Stephanie,
Marty / Amanda / Chase /
Craig / Vicky / Leslie /
Barry / Don and Karen Helms,
Ben and Brandon,

Word

2 Tim. 2:14 – *The Profane & Idle Babblings forbidden Anno.*

"Remind them of the things, charging them before the Lord not to strive about words to no profit, to the ruin of the hearers."

הזכר להם את הדברים האלה והזהר אותם לפני

האלהים שלא יתוכחו על דברים שאין בהם מועיל

ואינם אלא הורסים את השומעים

2 Tim. 2:19 – "2 of 2 marks1 of a true believer / Christian" Gal. 5:24 p.#M

"...let everyone who names the name of Christ depart iniquity."

אבל היסוד החזק

שהניח אלהים עומד איתן ויש לו החותם הזה

וידע יהוה את אשר לו וגם יסור מעול כל

הקורא בשם יהוה

Prayer

Lucretia Lewis,
Cindy Parsons,
Jud and Cindy,
Marty / Tiffany and Cole,
Lee / Debbie and Patrick Spiker,
Charlie, Doug, Scott, Jim,
Paul Larson, Peggy Sue,
Jimmy and Loretta,
Dan and Michelle,
Cory and Karen,
Randy Snell, Carl,
Bill Lujan, Karma, Debbie,
guy nickname "Rerun",
Eric nickname "Paladin",
guy who either called or
calls himself "Bummer",
Becky and Lyle Shwindt,
Harley and Gwen,
Jim Morse, Kelly,
Dirk Blackmor, Paco,

Word

2 Tim. 3: 2-5 – forbidden
"For men will be lovers of themselves, lovers of money, boasters, proud, blasphemers, disobedient to parents, unthankful, unholy, unloving, unforgiving, slanderers, without self-control, brutal, despisers of good, traitors, headstrong, haughty, lovers of pleasure rather than lovers of God, having a form of godliness but denying its power. And from such people turn away!"

כי יהיו האנשים אוהבי עצמם אוהבי כסף

גאותנים שחצנים מגדפים ממרים את פי

הוריהם כפויי טובה חסרי קדשה קשוחי לב

בלתי מתרצים מלשינים הוללים אכזרים שונאי

טוב בוגדים פוחזים יהירים אוהבים תענוגות

יותר משהם אוהבים את אלהים לכאורה בעלי

יראת שמים אך כופרים בתקפה התרחק מאלה

Prayer

<u>Kirk,</u>
<u>Sid nickname "Sid Vicious",</u>
<u>guy nickname "Red",</u>
<u>another guy nickname "Red",</u>
<u>William Scofield,</u>
<u>Buddy / Dillan / Charlie /</u>
<u>Dan / and Eric Piercall,</u>
<u>Scotty [Johnner],</u>
<u>Moment of Silence –</u>
<u>Eric and his dad Phillip,</u>
<u>John Hunt,</u>
<u>Philip who either</u>
<u>called or calls himself</u>
<u>"Lucifer",</u>
<u>Jerry who either</u>
<u>called or no longer called</u>
<u>"Crazy Jerry",</u>
<u>Dwain,</u>
<u>Jason [Ostricker],</u>
<u>Raylin Lenard,</u>
<u>Paula Carver,</u>
<u>Shane Shipply, Lyle Foster,</u>
<u>Robert Cross, Chris Oliver,</u>

Word

2 Tim. 3:12a – 1/2 persecution prophecy Anno.
"...literally to be hunted."

**2 Tim. 3:12b – 2/2 persecution prophecy / —Anno.
Matt. 24:22—**
"God does not promise us deliverance from persecution but deliverance through it."

"...Christians will not have to endure persecution forever..."

**Heb. 1: 7 – angels & [ministers] a flame of fire /
(righteousness & judgment) Anno.**
"...who makes His angels spirits And His ministers a flame of fire."

ועל המלאכים הוא אומר

עשה מלאכיו רוחות

משרתיו אש להט

Heb. 4:10 – Sabbath Holy rest requirement
"For he who has entered His rest has himself also ceased from his works as God did from His."

הן הנכנס אל מנוחתו גם הוא

שבת ממלאכתו כמו האלהים משלו

Prayer

Joey Burgen,
Mark Schumaucher,
Preston Gulley,
John Migee,
Kaleaha and Heather Veach,
Clint, Billy Peadon,
Lisa [O'Donald], Betty Runyan,
Mike Runyan,
Brian and Donna Bridges,
Mike Laccase, Matt, [Lestor],
Gina Hill, Bev Vasser,
Tammy, Tonya,
Danny Carson, Emily,
Katie Parish,
Shawn Kern,
Aaron Bateman,
Joanna and Christy,
Mindy Cline and Ali Stearns,
Keith Aipperspach,
Harvey and Rusty Crandall,
Steve, Jim Bond, Terry,

Word

Heb. 6:19 – Hope leads to Holiness requirement
"This hope we have as an anchor of the soul, both sure and steadfast, and which enters the Presence behind the veil..."

תקוה שהיא כעגן בטוח ויציב לנפשנו

ומגיעה אל מבית לפרכת

Heb. 10:23 – 6/6 Confession of Hope for rest Anno. [by mouth / not by mouth]
"Confession of our hope is the believer's confident expectation of the future. Promised here may refer to the promise of rest(4: 1)..."

Heb. 11: 1 – ("Faith Chapter") faith is substance
"Now faith is the substance of things hoped for, the evidence of things not seen."

האמונה היא בטחון בממשות הדברים

המקיים הוכחת דברים שאינם נראים

James 1:19 – hear fast / slow to speak / slow to anger / requirements
"So then, my beloved brethren, let every man be swift to hear, slow to speak, slow to wrath."

על כן אחי אהובי יהא כל איש מהיר לשמע

בלתי נחפז לדבר וקשה לכעס

James 2: 8-9 – favoritism forbidden Anno.

Prayer

<u>Tony either</u>
<u>called or calls herself</u>
<u>"Tone" and her brother</u>
<u>Tod Malleck,</u>
<u>John and Clint Turpen,</u>
<u>Jeremy Hanson,</u>
<u>Travis and Bonny Gladson,</u>
<u>Cindy and Howard, Aaron,</u>
<u>Waylan Rader, Chuck,</u>
<u>Brandi Austin,</u>
<u>Brian Williams,</u>
<u>Jesse and Tom Simons,</u>
<u>Jamie,</u>
<u>Dr. Zolcick, Dr. Lykes,</u>
<u>Dr. Patel, Dori Beck,</u>
<u>Bill Monahan,</u>
<u>Dale Burrer,</u>
<u>Janet Ballentyne and</u>
<u>Dwain Ballentyne,</u>
<u>Jim Tobin,</u>
<u>Scott and Deano and Amy,</u>
<u>Krystal Hendricks,</u>
<u>Geene Rudibush,</u>

Word

James 2:22 – Faith then Works requirements
"Do you see that faith was working together with his works, and by works faith was made perfect?"

רואה אתה כי

האמונה עזרה למעשיו ומתוך המעשים השלמה

האמונה

James 4:17 – he who knows to do good requirement
"Therefore, to him who knows to do good and does not do it, to him it is sin."

לכן היודע לעשות טוב ואיננו עושה לחטא

יחשב לו

James 5:16 – 4/6 Confessions of Sins circumstantial '(only one by mouth)'
"Confess your trespasses *to one another*, and pray for one another, that you may be healed..."

התודו על

חטאיכם איש לפני רעהו והתפללו איש בעד רעהו

למען תרפאו גדול כחה של תפלת צדיק בפעלתה

1 Peter 2: 5 – all believers are priests Anno. / Rev. 1: 4-6

"...all believer's are priests who have the privilege and responsibility of offering *spiritual sacrifices (Mark 10:45)* to God."

1 Peter 5: 5-6 – humility & humble requirements

2 Peter 3:12 – Fire of The Day of the Lord; Rapture's end of 2nd & 3rd heavens (universe & earth)

"...looking for and hastening the coming of the day of God, because of which the heavens will be dissolved, being on fire, and the elements will melt with fervent heat?(against the wicked)"

לחכות לבוא יום האלהים

ולהחיש אותו יום שבגללו השמים יתפרקו באש

והיסודות יבערו וימסו

Prayer

Bunny / Mary / Tracy /
Susie and Debbie Scott,
Kim and Sherry,
Mike and Sharon Trigg,
Amy and Scott Davis,
Misty Cummings,
Lyle Haberland, Candace,
Stuart and his dad,
Kim Hemphill, Bobby Jo,
Kris Riley, Sandy Phelps,
Justin Rosenau,
Kim Larson,
Jeremy and Nola Nelson,
Linda and Shelby and her
other children,
Liz, Karen,
Valerie and her husband,
Trish, Gus, Janet Happs,
Marty Rugar,
Evaune [Christene],
Gene, Larry, Loyd,
David Geer,

Word

1 John 1: 9 – 3/6 Confessions of Sins '(not by mouth)'
"If we confess our sins, He'(God)' is just to forgive'(God)' us our sins and to cleanse us from all unrighteousness."

אם נתודה על חטאינו נאמן הוא וצדיק לסלח

לנו על חטאינו ולטהר אותנו מכל עולה

1 John 2:15 – Do Not Love the "world" requirement

1 John 4:18 – There is no fear in love

1 John 5:17 – unrighteousness is sin forbidden
"All unrighteousness is sin, and there is sin not leading to death."

כל עולה חטא היא אך יש חטא

שאינו חטא-מות

1 John 5:18 – the "Born Again" does not sin
"We know that whoever is born of God does not sin; but he who has been born of God *keeps himself...*"

יודעים אנו כי כל מי שנולד

מאלהים איננו חוטא הוא אשר נולד מאלהים

שומר אותו והרע אינו נוגע בו

Prayer

[Jud] and Chad
nickname "Chatterbox",
[Darrall McGloffin],
Carmon, Chris,
Anita Larson, Ron [Louwers],
Bob Mitchell, Vince, Brad,
Mary, Kris, Dan Overman,
Juanita, Jack,
Wade Whetstone, George,
Bill Madson,
Tracy Bostick,
Scott Benson, Scott Swope,
Shawn Japp, Mike [Trexler],
Billy Wagner, Erin Morgan,
Sandra Slocum,
Ted and Juanita Higgs,
Scott Dommino,
Otis Eldridge,
JC Reynolds, Kandy,
Sara Cubbage, John Fleck,
Frankie, Joe Force,
Julie Murphy,
Judge Edwards,

Word

**Rev. 1: 4-6 – all believers are kings & priests Anno.
1 Peter 2: 5 *Mark 10:45***
"Christ's sacrifice set apart(made holy) believers as royal priests to offer *spiritual sacrifices* to God."

Rev. 1:20 – 7 stars, (angels(HS), lampstands, churches))

**Rev. 2:23 – Jesus searches the minds & hearts
Rev. 21: 5**
"...I am He who searches the minds and hearts."

אהרג במות את בניה וידעו כל

הקהלות שאני הוא הבוחן כליות ולב ואתן לכם

איש איש כמעשיכם

Rev. 3:11 – hold on to what you have requirement
"...hold fast what you have, that no one may take your crown."

אני בא מהר

החזק במה שיש לך כדי שאיש לא יקח את

העטרת שלך

Rev. 3:19 – zealous & repentance requirements
"...therefore be zealous and repent."

אני את אשר אהב

אוכיח ואיסר לכן היה נמרץ וחזר בתשובה

Prayer

Judge Wolf, Judge Deegan,
Cathy Edelman,
Felix Sewata,
Hunter Patrick,
Brad from "RENEW",
Zane from "RENEW",
Brian Coleman,
Jenny Stoner, Lenny,
guy who either
called or calls himself ["Axel"],
Mike Clemans,
Shawn Burns,
Bernie Sansusi,
James Mackelvain,
Lennette [Cooper],
Jason Roberts, Danny Cox,
Dale,
gal who either
called or calls herself
"Calamity Jane",
Keith and Brenda [Eden]
(possible relation),
Mike and Donella Pease,

Word

Rev. 7: 3 – Seal of God's servants prophecy
"...do not harm the earth, the sea, or the trees till we have sealed the servants of our God on our foreheads."

באמרו אל תחבלו בארץ ובים ובעצים

עד אשר נחתם את עבדי אלהינו על מצחותיהם

Rev. 13: 6 – he will appear to be victorious Anno.
"...he(Satan / Antichrist) will appear to be victorious over God's people."

**Rev. 13:10a – take captive, be captive
 (against believers) forbidden**
"He who leads into captivity, shall go into captivity."

המיעד לשבי ילך

בשבי והמיעד להרג בחרב יהרג בחרב בזה

סבלנות הקדושים ואמונתם

Rev. 13:10b – kill by sword, be killed by sword forbidden

"...he who kills with the sword must be killed with the sword..."

המיעד לשבי ילך

בשבי והמיעד להרג בחרב יהרג בחרב בזה

סבלנות הקדושים ואמונתם

Prayer

Bob Romero, Tyler,
Lucille / Bud / Dena / and
James Swain,
Jim Paden,
Duffy and DeeAnn Jenniges,
Reagan,
Phillip / Jean / and Randy Stahla,
Joe,
Peggy Hill, Maggy,
Judith Semple,
Shane Shaw, Curtis,
Colleen, Billy Mercer,
[Aliweesio], Mrs. Sorenson,
Chuck and Bo Rourke,
Linna and Bill Beebe,
AJ / Sharon / Emma / Sue / Jim and
Donna Cousins(AJ's previous),
[Dehauny], Tom Triplett,
Raylene, Gary Parker,
James Nalley,
JD(Quentin's friend),
Pat(Quentin's friend),
Andy(Quentin's friend),

Word

Rev. 13:16 – devils mark2 right hand or forehead forbidden (get a skin graph) p.#M

"He causes all '(unbelievers)', both small and great, rich and poor, free and slave, to receive a mark on the right hand or on their foreheads..."

והיא גורמת לכך שהכל

הקטנים והגדולים העשירים והעניים החפשיים

והעבדים ישימו להם תו על יד ימינם או על

מצחם

Rev. 13:17 – to buy or sell restriction prophecy

"And that no one may buy or sell except one who has the mark or the name of the beast, or the number of his name."

-כדי שלא יוכל איש לקנות או למכר

אלא מי שיש לו התו שם החיה או מספר שמה

Prayer

Brook and Grace,
Elizabeth and Keith,
Cody, Blake,
Tim and [Alana] Vangrinsvan,
Dave(therapist and friend),
Linda and Tim King,
Nick, Mari, Megan,
Martha, Amber, Rachel,
Monwello, Charlie,
Dale Kennedy, Alisha,
Wendy, Angela Mills,
Rebecka Danforth,
Melvin Ginest, Evee,
David Yarnel,
Rachel(from school), Willy,
Benny Hodges, [Robin],
Everett,
Sam Alexander, Austin,
Levi / [Sahara] and Everett,
Jade,
Dr. Lemerande, Dr. Billin,
Dr. Mary Khan, Dr. Mainini,

Word

Rev. 14: 4 – (purity), adoption, & Seal
Rom. 8:15 Rev. 7: 3

"These are the ones who were not defiled with women, for they are *virgins...*" *"(symbolic for purity)"*

אלה הם אשר לא נטמאו בנשים כי

בתולים הם אלה הם ההולכים אחרי השה לכל

אשר ילך אלה נפדו מבני אדם בכורים לאלהים

ולשה

Rev. 16:15 – Rapture prophecy
"Behold, I am coming as a thief."

הנני בא כגנב אשרי השוקד ושומר את

בגדיו פן ילך ערום ויראו את ערותו

Rev. 19:19 – war against Christ prophecy forbidden

Rev. 21: 5 – God makes all things new Rev. 2:23

Rev. 21: 7 – God's sons and daughters, brothers & sisters in Christ We are

Prayer

<u>Dr. Artrip, Dr. Cacares,</u>
<u>Brittney,</u>
<u>Tyler(Shane's neighbor),</u>
[Grechen],
Fred(Pastor Shane's dad by request),
Pastor Shane and his family by request,
<u>Jess and Rāchel,</u>
<u>August, Aunt Frona, Dewey,</u>
<u>Anderson, Carol, Nicole,</u>
<u>Sidney,</u>
<u>Levi Strickland,</u>
<u>Juanita Sapp,</u>
<u>Cecilia Yuanas(Yoon[a]s),</u>
<u>Charlotte Deming,</u>
<u>Eric Silk,</u>
<u>Shantelle,</u>
<u>David, Jim, Chelsy, Tina,</u>
"Joey, Pat, Piper,
Macey George,
'Little Lilly,
Mary Merke,

Word

Rev. 21: 8 – forbidden
"But the cowardly, unbelieving, abominable, murderers, sexually immoral, sorcerers'witchcraft', idolaters, and all liars, shall have their part in the lake which burns with fire and brimstone..."

אבל מוגי הלב והבלתי מאמינים המתעבים

והמרצחים הזונים והמכשפים עובדי האלילים

וכל המשקרים – חלקם באגם הבוער באש וגפרית

אשר הוא המות השני

Rev. 21:27 – the Lamb's Book of Life / Water of Life / Tree of Life Rev. 22:14, 17
"...there shall by no means enter it anything that defiles, or causes an abomination or a lie, but only those who are written in the Lamb's Book of Life."

ולא יכנס

אליה כל טמא ועושה תועבה ושקר כי אם

הכתובים בספר החיים של השה

Prayer

Sandra Bennett / Ron / and
Steve, Lou,
Scottie and Kali,
Hazel and Randy, Mark",
<u>Kristy, Heather,</u> [Susan /
Talon / Alanan(ᵃlănăn) /
            ]<u>Anthoney</u>"],
Sawyer's dad / <u>Sawyer,
John, John, Diana, Diane,
Larry Ostermiller, Bill, Pam,
a young lady I call
'the second girl',
a woman prophet
by the name of
Julia and her husband,
Brett McCoy / Stella / Jeff and
family,
Elizabeth Ventura,
Ryan and [Vanessa],
Deb, Kari(kerri), Steve, John,</u>
Kim Mauthe by request,

Word

Rev. 22:14 – the Gates of Heaven & the Lamb's Book of Life

"Blessed are those who do His commandments, that they may have the right to the tree of life, and may enter through the gates into the city."

אשרי המכבסים את גלימותיהם למען תהיה

להם זכות על עץ החיים ויכנסו העירה דרך

השערים

Rev. 22:18-19 – Neither add nor take away from the Bible forbidden Prov. 30:v6

'All headings not word for word; all scripture is word for word(original).'

200 scriptures are average for most ministers to memorize.

Prayer

Tomas,
Kris,
Ken,
Rhonda and family by request,
Corinne [Kiehn],
Phillip(also for peace and quiet for Phillip) by request,
Nathan,
Cheralyn,
Shea,
James Russell,
Adreanna,
Brenda Good by request,
Kathy,
Pat,
Shawna,
Alānān,
George,
Rich,
Austin West,
Tim,
Greg,
Heidi Johnson,
Bonnie,
[Dr. Brackett],
[Jordanna],
Michelle,
Pat,

<u>Ashley,</u>
<u>Mary,</u>
<u>Jeff,</u>
<u>Dr. William Jarvis,</u>
<u>President Trump and his family,</u>
<u>the O-zone layer,</u>
<u>the earth,</u>

Proclamation

Deut. 33:25-37(NIV)-
"The bolts of our gates will be iron and bronze, and our strength will equal your days. There is no one like the God of Jeshurun, who rides on the heavens to help you and on the clouds in His majesty. The eternal God of our refuge, and underneath are the everlasting arms. He will drive out our enemy before us, saying, "Destroy him!"

Luke 21:36 – watch, stay awake(figuratively), & pray prayer Matt. 26:38
"Watch therefore, and pray always that you may be counted worthy to escape all these things that will come to pass, and to stand before the Son of Man."

לכן עמדו על

המשמר בכל עת והתפללו שיהיה בכחכם להמלט

מכל העתידות האלה ולהתיצב לפני בן-האדם

Heb. 11:33-35 – from the Faith Chapter
"Who through faith conquered kingdoms, worked righteousness, obtained promises, stopped the mouths of lions, Quenched the violence of fire, escaped the edge of the sword, out of weakness were made strong, became valiant in battle, turned to flight the armies of the aliens, Women received their dead raised to life again..."

Prayer

...

Proclamation

Rev. 1: 4-6 –
"...grace to you and peace from Him who is and who was and who is to come, and from the seven Spirits who are before His throne, and from Jesus Christ, the faithful witness, the firstborn from the dead, and the ruler over the kings of the earth. To Him who loved us and washed us from our sins in His own blood, and has made us kings and priests to His God and Father, to Him be glory and dominion forever and ever. Amen."

יוחנן אל שבע הקהלות אשר באסיה חסד

ושלום לכם מאת ההוה והיה ויבוא ומאת שבע

הרוחות אשר לפני כסאו ומאת ישוע המשיח

העד הנאמן בכור המתים ועליון למלכי הארץ

לאוהב אותנו אשר בדמו שחרר אותנו מחטאינו

ועשה אותנו ממלכת כהנים לאלהים אביו לו

הכבוד והגבורה לעולמי עולמים אמן

Prayer

...

Proclamation

Saint Michael – "St. Michael the Archangel defend us in battle, be our protection against the wickedness and snares of the devil, may God rebuke him we humbly pray, and do thou O prince of the Heavenly hosts, by the divine power of God Cast into Hell⁻ Satan and all evil spirits who wander through-out the world, who seek the ruin of souls", in the name of the Father and of the Son and of the Holy Spirit, Amen.

Prayer

...

Legitimate Vocabulary

A/
- Abba – Heb. For Father
- Aborigines – men who survive w/o materials
  - Neanderthals – 'men who survive on love'
- Abraham's Bosom – a good place of confinement
  - Sheol –
  - Hades –
  - Purgatory –
- accent – diff. talk diff. Area
  - dialect – diff. talk diff. time
  - lingo – same meaning diff. word
- accountable – minister's job
- acid reflux "cure' 1 – not heart burn; drink & eat separate 20 min. between
- acolyte – minister's helper
- acronym – 'one design of more than one'
- a cry for justice – "in Jesus' name"
- active duty – war duty
- adopted – by the HS Rom. 8:15
- adrenaline –
  - accupen – an antidote against bee stings
- adultery – forbidden; forgivable
  - spiritual adultery – hab. sexual imagination
- aerobic – toning by heart-rate

anaerobic – muscle building
affection – expression of love
  'effection' – effect of love
alien – foreigner [or ET?]
alleged(supposed) – dirty phrase for supposed
allergies1&2 – possible death w/o treatment
ally – friend
  adversary – foe

Prayer

...

Legitimate Vocabulary

A/
- annotations – bible notes
  - notes –
  - footnotes –
  - glosses –
- annulled – "putting away" of L/law by repentance & love
- apostasy – abandoned faith
- apostle – one sent
  - missionary –
- Archangel – commander of angels
- Archbishop – head bishop; [not Pope]
- Archives(WashingtonDC) – records of [Americans]
- argue – forbidden
  - correction – requirement when needed only
- Armors –
  - Gifts –
  - Fruits –
  - Church Qualities –
- arrival – [at destination]
  - departure – [at take-off]
- arthritis treatment – prescription NSAID, Alpha Lipoic Acid, exercise surrounding area
- asceticism – denying oneself for another
- "assault & battery" –
- asthma – emergency inhaler etc.

atonement – Christ took our sins upon Him-
             self
  ransom – "bought with blood" we are
attachments – addictions(idols)
attitude; good… – requirement
*authority – inflicts pain legally,
             it is wrong
  Authority – fair and merciful

Prayer

...

Legitimate Vocabulary

B/

    Babylonian – old language [before] the flood
    Bĕătitudes – Eccl. 3: 9, Matt. 5, Luke 6:20
            "Sermon on the Mount"
    begging – for needs; (Catholic Franciscans)
    benign – harmless
    biological family – family by birth
       Christian family – family by Christ
    bishop –
    blasphemy(profane) – to curse habitually
                      forbidden
    bleach – carcinogen; [8 to 10] drops per gal.
       Chlorine Dioxide – even safer to drink w/ wtr.
    blocked intestines –
    Body1 – flesh & bones(church)
       Body2 – sanctified building(church)
    bosom – [heart-felt]
    breath(breathe) – life
       blood – soul
    Buddhism – Satanism
    bulk foods – "premium bulk foods"
               (human food)

    buying & selling – hab. greed & attachment
       catalogs – especially
       television – mostly has evil
       radio – mostly idle talk
    bypass – go around
       reinforce – adding strength
       process of elimination – mechanic methods

Prayer

...

Legitimate Vocabulary

C/

  cadence – military marching songs
  cancer prevent1 – avoid toxins
  cancer prevent2 – aspirin; flavonoids,
                   green tea, grapeseed extract
  cancer1 – carrot juice(beta)
  cancer2 – cancer center
  cancer3(infoonly) – Lymphocytes(intravenously)
  cancer4(infoonly) – Interferon(balanced)
                  (alpha, beta, gamma))
  Canonize1 – record of some saints
    Canonize2 – record of bible text
  car-pooling – fast lane driving w/ less
            than 2 people
  car sale sign – use shoe polish
  CEO – boss/chief executive officer
  chastity – self-discipline requirement
        (not specifically sex)
    bored – a demon
  Christian –
    children of God – "foolishness of God is
                  more wise than the
                  wisdom of man"
    Christian family – church family
    Christian disciple –
  Christian Sabbath – Sunday
    Jewish Sabbath – Saturday
  Christian Schools – private school costs;
                 but I recommend it

Church1 –
- flesh & bones – w/ HS 1 Cor. 12:27-28
- [Body of Christ] – flesh & bones w/ HS
- temple – flesh & bones w/ HS
- Body1; the… – flesh and bones w/ HS

Church2 –
- Bride of Christ – sanctified building
- [Bride of Christ] – sanctified building
- Body2; the… – sanctified building
- [Eucharist2]; the… – sanctified building

Prayer

I pray for all or any of the P/people
   who put together the
—"New King James Versions",
   all or any of the P/people
   who put together the
—"Holman Illustrated
   Bible Dictionary"(HIBD),
—Peter Derek Vaughn Prince and
   all or any of the others
   who put together
   "Derek Prince Ministries",
—"Sarah Nicholson
   teach yourself Hebrew",
   all or any of the P/people
   who put together the
—"Zondervan" company,
   all or any of the P/people
   who put together the
—"Shula Gilboa
   teach yourself modern Hebrew",
   all or any of the P/people
   who put together the
—"biblegateway.com
   website",
   all or any of the P/people
   who put together the

—"Webster's Dictionaries",
I pray for
   who and whoever,
   what and whatever,
   all those around me,
   all those who know me,
   all those who knew me,
   all kinds of witnesses of Jesus,

Legitimate Vocabulary

C/

   coal – no vines($200. Pick-up truck)
   "collateral" – "something given as
                a pledge for repayment"
   Communion – reenactment of the
              Last Supper requirement
              (unless confessed)
    "Confirmation" – "HS by baptism"
   concubine – 2nd wife most status
   conditions – Bible rules reasonably rewarded
   "conflict of interest" –
    "disorderly conduct" – yes, I know
   contemplative prayer – spontaneous prayer
   context – used for interpretation
   control-freak – civil blasphemy
     over-qualified –
     over-confident –
   Convent – nun monastery
   convict2(c^{a}nvict) – convince;
                   only in context
   cooperating w/ demons – forbidden
   Cornerstone – [the Church]
     Foundation – Jesus
   correction – Christian requirement
            only as needed
     rebuke –
     reproof –
     reprove –

crohn's disease cure1 – drink first, eat 20 min. later always
crohn's disease cure2 – prescription probiotic
cross reference – related ref. from elsewhere literally

Prayer

for the Bible and
for this book,
for accomplishments and
to go home,
for myself and
everything we need?
In the name of
Jesus Christ the Son of God,
Amen

I hope, I pray, and I ask
 10 Prayers including One Invocation and
 or Invitation for Embodiment for everybody
 and the chosen and or adopted by the HS;
 against Satan and demons, and [pandemic,

 ],

 don't ask me to quote this but,
 in reference to
 Rev. 14: 4, Rom. 8:15, Rev. 7: 3 –
Saint Gabrielx1 – St. Gabriel
 "the Archangel defend us
 in battle, be our protection
 against the wickedness and
 snares of the devil,
 may God rebuke him we humbly
 pray, and do thou O Prince
 of the Heavenly hosts, by
 the divine power of God
 Cast into Hell Satan and
 all evil spirits who wander
 through-out the world,

who seek the ruin of souls",
in the name of the
Father and of the Son and
of the Holy Spirit, Amen.

Legitimate Vocabulary

D/
   darn-it – civil blasphemy
      dang-it –
      I'll be darn –
      gosh dang-it –
      dab blam-it –
   deacon – minister's helper
   death1 – the demon
      Death2 – the place
   debriefing – military word for taking notes
      'journaling' –
      reconnaissance – from the field
      recon –
   decency – requirement
      order – requirement
   decline2 – gentleman's way of saying no
   "deductible" – paying lump sum before coverage
   deficiency – nutrient deprived etc.
   dehydrated food – dried vacuumed food
      freeze-dried food – dried by freezing survivalists choice
   deliverance prayer –
      exōrcise(escape) – means escape in Hebrew
      exōrcism –
      ekballo – Greek
      casting out and casting away –

    exposing demons(not people) –
    taking Ground2 – the Godhead takes all
               because He gives all
demons – are spirits
   humans – humans aren't demons
   spirits – demons and humans

Prayer

<u>Saint Michael x1</u> – "St. Michael the Archangel defend us in battle, be our protection against the wickedness and snares of the devil, may God rebuke him we humbly pray, and do thou O Prince of the Heavenly hosts, by the divine power of God Cast into Hell⁻ Satan and all evil spirits who wander through-out the world, who seek the ruin of souls", in the name of the Father and of the Son and of the Holy Spirit, Amen.

Legitimate Vocabulary

D/

  denominational – strict and forbidden
    nondenominational – not strict; required
  deploy – send troops
  diploma – education required,
             strictness forbidden
    degree – college
  direct1 – way of explaining scripture
    indirect1 –
  dirty1 – (a)uthority; not (A)uthority
  discernings of S/spirits – sensing S/spirits
                      (mysticism)
  disciple; Christian… – follower of Christ
  "disclosure" – required information
  "disorderly conduct" –
    "conflict of interest" – yes, I know
  dispatch – police receptionist
  divine exchange – transfer from Jesus for
                  HS
  doctrine(teachings) –
  double minded – two souls
  dragon – Satan; unHoly trinity
    beast – Antichrist(s)
    false prophet – False prophet(s)
  dynasty – a successful family

Prayer

<u>Holy Maryx3</u> – 'Holy Mary?",
"Hail Mary, full of grace.
The Lord is with thee.
Blessed art thou among
women, and blessed is
the fruit of thy womb,
Jesus. Holy Mary,
Mother of God,
pray for us sinners, now
and at the hour of our
death"
in the name of the
Father and of the Son and
of the Holy Spirit, Amen.
<u>Jesusx1</u> – 'Holy Lord
Jesus Christ the Son of
God?',
The Spirit of the Lord shall
rest upon Him,
'I pray for'
the Spirit of Wisdom and
Understanding,
the Spirit of Counsel

Legitimate Vocabulary

E/

   Ears, Nose, and Throat – Otolaryngology
   edification – a sober drunk feeling
     "building up" – edification
   El Nino – "The Boy" refers to earth's
          volcanic surface temperature
   endure – survive faithfully
     perseverance –
     improvise –
     adapt & overcome –
   enmity(bitterness) –
   "entrapment" –
   epistle – a letter
   <u>etching – complete original piece</u>
        (<u>makes copies</u>)
   Evangelical – salvation by faith
     Orthodox – established doctrines
     Nondenominational – not under L/law
              but under grace
     Nonsectarian – not under a religion but
            under God
   "excessive force" – brutalities
   excommunication – banned from
               Church(es)
   "expedite"(stat, asap) –
   "extortion" – stealing money(etc.)
            by force or threat

eye infections cure1 – (infoonly) splash eyeballs w/ almost hot water
eye infections cure2 – (infoonly) salt water eyedrops(.09% ratio), only about a couple of times
eye infections cure3 – (infoonly)antibiotics; 2 weeks to a month

Prayer

And Might,
The Spirit of knowledge
and of the fear of the
Lord, in reference to
Isaiah 11: 2
in the name of the
Father and of the Son and
of the Holy Spirit, Amen.
Holy Spiritx1 – (DPM, lost, or
unclaimed / Sept. 2016) probably
intended to Jesus; but
this one is indicated to the
Holy Spirit))-
Holy Spirit?,
the seven Spirits of God?,
I invoke and or invite thee
for Embodiment.
"If You were knocking on the
door of my heart?
If You were calling me
by name asking me to
open the door of my
heart to You?
'Holy Spirit', I open

Legitimate Vocabulary

F/

    faith & works – requirements
    fantasy – demon if hab.
    fat – a dirty word for over-weight;
        blasphemy
    fatigue – can't sleep, can't stay awake
      insomnia – chronic sleeplessness
    fight, flight, freeze – secular survival
    flank – blind attack(from any direction)
    flesh1 – describes a person(body)
      flesh2 – describes a "church(body)"
    follow-through – "self-defense"
    foolish – blasphemy on earth forbidden
        Matt. 5:22
    former – before
      latter – after
    Freemasons – "false religion,
                fraternal order"
    free-will – restriction
      God's will – requirement
    freeze-dried – survivalists food of choice
      dehydrated – food
    frequency reader – can measure smallest
                    of things

Prayer

the door of my heart to
You by this prayer of commit-
ment.
Come in to my life in a
fresh new way.
If I have kept You
from any area of my
life, I break down all
the barriers of Your entry
with this prayer
of invitation.
Come in 'Holy Spirit', come
in. You are welcome here in
my heart 'and mind'.
I look forward to dining
with You, and spending
time in fellowship in
ways that I have not
experienced before.
Thank You for knocking
on the door of my heart,
I thank You for calling

Legitimate Vocabulary

G/

  genealogy –
    ancestors –
    descendants –
  genuflect – Catholic for kneeling
  Gingivitis treatment1 – floss after brushing not before
  Gingivitis treatment2 – "oil or water pulling"
  "Gingivitis cure1 – antibiotics"
  give-up – don't give-up
    give-in – give-in to God Who cares
  God & Man – Jesus
  "God created the earth and all the good things in it" –
  "God / man race" – Jesus to today
    "Adamic race" – Adam to Jesus
    "pre-Adamic race" – diff. races before Adam
  Godhead(Heaven's Entities) –
  Godly –
    unGodly("hypocrite") –
  good – only God is Good context(:)
  good works – requirement
    dead works – forbidden
  gospel – good news preaching
    fire & brimstone – Hell⁻ fire preaching
  "grace period" –
  greasy clothes – saturate w/ hot water and brush/rub w/ Palmolive, rinse

Prayer

me by name",
I invoke and or invite thee
for Embodiment
in the name of the
Father and of the Son and
of the Holy Spirit, Amen.
Lord's Prayerx3 – The Lord's
prayer;
Our Father in Heaven,
Hallowed be thy name
Your kingdom come.
Your will be done
on earth as it is in
Heaven.
Give us this day our
daily bread.
And forgive us our debts,
As we forgive our
debtors,
And do not lead us into
temptation,
But deliver us from the
evil one. For Your's

Legitimate Vocabulary

H/
- habitual – demonic
  - non-habitual – not demonic
- hades1 – the demon
  - Hades2 – the place
- "harassment" – law helps against harassment
  - "badgering" – law doesn't help against badgering
  - "stalking" –
- hate – forbidden
- heading – describes bible content
- heed(attention) – requirement
- heist –
- Hell("2nd D/death") –
  - lake of fire –
  - bottomless pit of lake of fire –
- hepa filter – airborne mold/particles remover
  - gas filter – filters particles and gas
- HepatitisC cure – "Harvoni", "Mavyret"
- heretic – against church teaching
- Herod[   ] – bad king
- hollering – habit(vexation)
  - yelling –
  - screaming –
  - wrath –
- Holy Hour – "3:00pm"
  - "witching hour" – "3:00am" / "Midnight"

holy rollers – [   ]
Holy Spirit(HS) –
   Angel of the Lord –
   Spirit of God –
   the seven Spirits of God –
Holy Trinity –
   unHoly trinity – satanic trinity

Prayer

is the kingdom
and the power and the
glory forever,
in the name of the
Father and of the Son and
of the Holy Spirit, Amen.

Legitimate Vocabulary

H/
   hope – essential requirement
      dove – "sign of hope"
   host – serving God
      servant –
   House Rules1of3 – evil thoughts to a
                           minimum at least
   House Rules2of3 – no threatening
   House Rules3of3 – no killing
   "humanity law" –
   humble – no status requirement
      supplications –
   humility(reserved) – not humiliation
   [Hutterites] – Lutheran
      [Mennonites] –
      Amish – 'exclusion, inclusion, and or
              seclusion;
              not isolation'
      Quakers – vows of silence
              ("society of friends")
   hyphen – [–]
      dash – [-]
   hyssop(hissup) – anti-viral used in
                       Passover
                       (externally not internally)

Prayer

<u>Special Note2(Note)-</u>
  <u>Skip and go to</u>
  <u>'Effection to Affection' p.# 220</u>
  <u>Unless you know Hebrew or if</u>
  <u>you are ready to learn Hebrew?</u>
  <u>Hebrew is the original language</u>
  <u>of most of the OT</u>
  <u>Holy Bible's manuscripts,</u>
  <u>makes a beautiful meditation.</u>

Reciting<u>(unfold hands of prayer)</u>
  <u>Hebrew alphabet</u>
  <u>in English(to start with))-</u>
  a
  b
  g...

Legitimate Vocabulary

I/

   idle talk – <u>key word "fun"</u>; to make fun of,
               complain, & or negative talk
     carnal tongue –
     words that tear down
   idol – other gods forbidden
     idol worship – forbidden and
                harshly forgiven
   "If you can't take it don't dish it out" –
   "If your not prepared your never prepared" –
   ignorance1 – lack of knowledge
   ignorance2 – embarrassment
   "illicit" – "illegal"
   "immunity" – "special permission to make
               mistakes"
   in vain1 – cursing God forbidden
   in vain2 – doing works against God
            forbidden
   incompetent – incapable
   infirmity – deformity
   iniquity(wickedness) –
   intercession – standing for God and man
   "invasion of privacy" –
   invocation – to invite Spirits with prayer
     invitation –
     indwell –
     embodiment –
   Israel(the Holy Land) –

Prayer

d
h
v
v
z
ch
ch
t
y
k
l
m
n
s
ts(silent)
f
p
ts
k
r
s
sh...

Legitimate Vocabulary

J/
   jealousy –
   Jerusalem –
     Salem –
     the Holy City –
     she, her – Jerusalem
   Jesus – God's Son born from a virgin
   Jews("brothers of Jesus") – p.# 510
   "just(justice)" – fairness is the definition

Prayer

t.

—Hebrew alphabet in
English to English
("Idiomatic transliteration"), &
pronunciation))-
a / Aleph(ālĕf)
b / Beth(bayt)
g / Gimel(gēmayl)
d / Daleth(dālĕt)
h / He(hay)
v / Waw(wāw)
v / Waw(wāw)
z / Zayin(zayin)
ch / Kaf(chăf)
ch / Heth(hayt)
t / Teth(tayt)
y / Yod(yōd)
k / Kaph(kăf)
l / Lamed(lāmĕd)
m/ Mem(maym)
n/ Nun(noon)
s / Samek(sāmāch)
ts / Ayin(ăyin) silent))
f / Pe(fay)
p / Pe(pay)
ts / Tsadde(tsădē)
k / Quph(qōf)

r / Resh(raysh)
s / Shin(seen)
sh / Shin(sheen)
t / Tau(tāf)

Legitimate Vocabulary

K/
   knowledge – requirement /
               strictness forbidden though

Prayer

—Hebrew alphabet in
English to Hebrew –
a / א
b / בּ
g / ג
d / ד
h / ה
v / ו
v / ב
z / ז
ch / ח
ch / כ
t / ט
y / י
k / כּ
l / ל
m / מ
n / נ
s / ס
ts / ע(silent)
f / פ
p / פּ
ts / צ
k / ק
r / ר
s / שׂ
sh / שׁ
t / ת

Legitimate Vocabulary

L/
Law – Law not law; God's Law
   law – law not Law; man's law
lĕavĕn –
"left out of the loop" – secular phrase
legalism(strictness) – forbidden
Legion – 3500 to 4500 roman soldiers &
        or demons or Spirits
"legislation" – law makers
legitimate – reasonable and fair
   legit –
likeness of God – requirement
   God's not gay – "God takes no pleasure
               in the legs of a man"
Limbo – a heaven for animals;
       an actual place
living faith – requirement
   dead faith –
living water(water of life) – miracle water
long conversations w/ demons – forbidden
love overrides –
   love never fails – 1 Cor. 13: 8
Lucifer – Satan before he sinned w/ pride

Prayer

—Hebrew alphabet in
Hebrew to Hebrew, &
pronunciation –

אָלֶף / א

בֵּית / ב

גִימֶל / ג

דָלֶת / ד

הֵא / ה

וָו / ו

וָו / ב

זַיִן / ז

חֵית / ח

כָף / כ

טֵית / ט

יוֹד / י

כַּף / כּ

Legitimate Vocabulary

M/
- maltreatment – perversion
  - mischievous (mis-ch^a-v^{a}s) – menace
- manipulation – evil
  - intimidation – evil
  - domination – evil
- mark1 – not mark of the beast
  - mark2 – mark of the beast
  - Seal – seal of the 12 tribes
- marvel (wonder) –
- mayor – city utilities
- means – God's given ability
  - instruments – using our flesh as God's given ability
- Mecca – attachment; usually not healthy
- mercy killing – could be murder
- midlife crisis –
  - shortcomings –
- military alphabet (phonetic alphabet) –
- minister –
  - pastor –
  - clergyman –
  - preacher –
  - priest –
  - chaplain –
  - rabbi –

Prayer

לָמֶד / ל

מֵם / מ

נוּן / נ

סָמֶךְ / ס

עַיִן / ע

פֵּא / פ

פֵא / פ

צָדִי / צ

קוֹף / ק

רֵישׁ / ר

שִׁין / שׁ

שִׂין / שׂ

תָף / ת

Legitimate Vocabulary

M/
   "father" – Catholic falsehood Matt. 23: 9
   reverend –
modest –
monk –
Morning Star – Jesus, [   ]
morning thought – best times for thinking
   night-time thought – & meditation
mortified – requirement
   "fear of the Lord" – same thing
moss – has good iodine
motive2(love) – for successful prayer &
                works
Mt. Of Olives – Christ's ascension &
              2nd coming[in Syria]
myrrh(m^{a}r) – incense & anti-septic
          depends on consistency

Prayer

Reciting "The Five Final Forms" –
1. ch / ך

2. m / ם

3. n / ן

4. f / ף

5. ts / ץ

Reciting '[The Seven Gutturals including the one alike]' <u>diff. pronunciation & takes a complex sheva(composite vowels)</u>-
1. a / א

2. h / ה

3. ch / ח

4. ch / כ

5. ch / ך

6. ts / [ע(silent) not צ]

and sometimes...

7. r / ר

Legitimate Vocabulary

N/
- nationality – biological origin
- natural Love –
  - Spiritual Love –
  - Divine Love –
  - Holy Love –
  - Agape Love –
- Net_2 – financing total after deductions
  - $Gross_2$ – financing total before deductions
- nitrites & nitrates – fertilizer [carcinogen / vitamin]
  - phosphorous –
- "no fly list" –
- "non-compliment$_1$" – dishonest w/ meds.
  - voluntary$_1$ – <u>free ride home</u>
  - involuntary$_1$ – <u>expect more counseling</u>
- nutrition facts –

Prayer

Reciting '[The Five Categories of the Twenty-Seven Vowels]' –
1. short vowels

2. long vowels

3. [shēvā or shēwā vowels]

4. [composite shēvā or shēwā vowels]

5. combination vowels

Reciting '[The Three Definite Articles]' for the word "the" which is –
1. hă

2. hĕ

and…

3. hā

spelled…
1. הַ

2. הֱ

3. הָ

Legitimate Vocabulary

O/
   obstacle course – for fitness
   'ocean glacier' – hits shore-lines
   ocean subway – underwater England to France
   "One man's poison is another man's cure" –
   "One man's cure is another man's poison" –
   ordain[1] – HS / Church makes ministers
     commission – HS / Church makes apostles(missionaries)
   ordinance(ordain[1]) – nondenominational
    *<order – nondenominational
    obedience(merciful) – non-denominational
    "sacrament" – denominational strictness, strictness forbidden
   OT – Old Testament
    NT – New...
   OTC – Over The Counter
   oxygen(infoonly) – OTC(ABO) or med. oxy.
    earth's oxygen – 21%

*derived from

Prayer

Reciting '[Five Conjunctions for the word "and" or "but"(find by context)]' –
  1. וְ / vᵃ and [v]

  2. וּ / [voo] and oo

  3. וִ / vi

  4. וֶ / vă

  5. וָ / vā

Reciting '[Four Inseparable Prepositions]' –
  1. בְּ / b = in / with

  2. כְּ / k = as / like

  3. לְ / l = to / at / for

  4. מִ / m = from

Legitimate Vocabulary

P/
- parable – story by metaphor w/ "moral to the story"
  - metaphor – meaning more than 1 thing
  - symbolic – 'code'
  - common sense – face value
- parentheses – ( )
- passions & desires – restrictions; forbidden
- pattern – being an example
  - setting an example –
- [peer(s)1] – church members
  - [peer(s)2] – church benches
- period – .
- persecution – "to be hunted not forever"
- petition(s) – prayer to Jesus to God
- phantom – black ghost
- Phillip the Evangelist –
- phonetic alphabet (military alphabet) –
- phrase –
- physical therapy –
- pilot hole – drilling a hole for a nail etc.
- pious – *Bible piety vs.* catholic piety
  Col. 2:20
  - piously – being pious
  - piety – a true or false form of an obedient way of life
  - regiment2 – discipline...

"policies" – the hidden print
               (only avail. by the asking)
polygamy – more than 1 spouse
polysaccerides – green tea,
                 grapeseed extract
pope – "head of Church"
positive lie – forbidden
  negative lie – forbidden
"power of attorney" –
praise – "God's Courts" '(courtier)'

Prayer

Reciting the Hebrew word for "to"
"indicating possession" is ל

Reciting a form of Azan but in
English, not Arabic
Deut. 32: 1, Deut. 5: 1b, & Ps. 130:v2 –
Give ear, O heavens,
and I will speak;
And hear O earth,
the words of my mouth
Hear, O Israel, the
Statutes and judgments
in which I speak
in your hearing today,
that you may learn them
and be careful to
observe them
Lord, hear my voice!
Let Your ears be
attentive
To the voice of my
supplications([humble]).

Reciting the above form of Azan
in Hebrew–...

הַאֲזִינוּ הַשָּׁמַיִם

וַאֲדַבֵּרָה וְתִשְׁמַע

הָאָרֶץ אִמְרֵי-פִי

שְׁמַע יִשְׂרָאֵל

אֶת-הַחֻקִּים

וְאֶת-הַמִּשְׁפָּטִים

אֲשֶׁר אָנֹכִי דֹּבֵר

בְּאָזְנֵיכֶם הַיּוֹם

וּלְמַדְתֶּם אֹתָם

וּשְׁמַרְתֶּם לַעֲשֹׂתָם

אֲדֹנָי שִׁמְעָה

בְקוֹלִי תִּהְיֶינָה

אָזְנֶיךָ קַשֻּׁבוֹת

לְקוֹל תַּחֲנוּנָי :

Legitimate Vocabulary

P/

pray – to ask
   "crying out" – done alone w/ God usually
   worship – to pray desperately
prayer list – list of people to pray for
"pre-Adamic race" – diff. races before Adam
   "Adamic race" – Adam to Jesus
   "God / man race" – Jesus to today
prefab – custom delivery
   modular –
prejudice – a spirit(demon)
   bias – civil blasphemy
   bigot – 'blasphemic'
premium1 – the best of a product
   premium2 – money down as a payment
pride – arrogant forbidden
   power – restriction
principalities&powers – demons; / angels, 2nd heaven(universe)
probiotic – against anything from a cold to crohn's disease
   prebiotic – [fiber]
process of elimination – a method for troubleshooting
proclamation(proclaim) – pray aloud
prophet – true prophet
   false prophet(s) –

prophesy – current prophecy
"protection & advocacy" – <u>PAIMI Program</u>
  "[legal aide]" – [state appointed attorney]
"protocol" – [new legislation]; oppression2
psychological warfare – war is war
psychology – doctrine from Antichrist falsehood
  Satanism – doctrine from Satan
  Humanism – doctrine from Antichrist
  "Human Resources(HR)" – via Antichrist
  Bible – doctrine from God
punctuation –
purifying faith – (:   )
pyramids; the… – a fortress might have more to
             it than that

Prayer

The Lord's Prayer in Hebrew –

אָבִינוּ שֶׁבַּשָּׁמַיִם

יִתְקַדֵּשׁ שְׁמֶךָ:

תָּבוֹא מַלְכוּתְךָ יֵעָשֶׂה

רְצוֹנְךָ כְּבַשָּׁמַיִם כֵּן

בָּאָרֶץ:

אֶת לֶחֶם חֻקֵּנוּ תֵּן

לָנוּ הַיּוֹם:

וּסְלַח לָנוּ עַל

חֲטָאֵינוּ כְּפִי

שֶׁסּוֹלְחִים

גַּם אֲנַחְנוּ לַהֹטְעִים

לָנוּ:

וְאַל תְּבִיאֵנוּ לִידֵי

נִסָּיוֹן כִּי אִם

הַצִּילֵנוּ מִן הָרָע:

Legitimate Vocabulary

Q/
   quality time – no such thing; life is quality
   quote – " " or ' '

Prayer

Prayer Again(fold hands of prayer)-
Effection to Affection
("The Gate")-
I pray and I love you St. Gabriel
  the Archangel,
  I love you St. Michael
  the Archangel,
  I love You Holy Mary,
  I love You and I thank You
  Holy Lord Jesus Christ
  the Son of God,
  I love You Holy Spirit,
  I love You the
  Holy Lord God the Father
  who loves us
  in Jesus' name
  Holy, Holy, Holy,
Sign of the Cross –
  in the name of the
  Father and of the Son and
  of the Holy Spirit, Amen.
Affection –(a whisper or less)...

... I love Y/you

Legitimate Vocabulary

R/

   rack&pinion – horizontal steering bar w/
                    vertical 'worm' gear
                    (power & or manual steering)
   radiation[cure] – nuclear; treatment—
     (fall-out) (potassium iodide, or
               vitamin C, or salt)
   răton – [sparing] food
   realm of time –
     realm of Eternal –
     time and Eternal –
   rebate – a set reimbursement from a
          purchase
   Recalls(health) – "several knee & hip
                    replacements
                    1-800-509-3360",
               Dēpuy knee replacement,
               Austin eye injections,
               Smith&Nephew
               Birmingham hip replace-
               ment 1-800-418-5116,
               class actions—
               simvastatin,"
   reckon – suppose
   reconciliation(reconcile) – [friendship]
   refinement(refine) – God's way to make
                    Christians

Prayer

PRONUNCIATION KEY –			
(Hebrew to English Vowels)			
Short Vowels			
pat	ă	־	1
set	ĕ	ֶ	2
sit	ī	ִ	3
hot	ŏ/ā	ָ	4
put	u	ֻ	5
Long Vowels			
blah	ā/ŏ	ָ	6
say	ay	ֵ	7
see	ee	׳ִ	8
go	ō	וֹ	9
zoo	oo	וּ	10
tomato	(a)	ֲ	11
set	(e)	ֱ	12
(silent)	(ˤ)	ְ	13

Legitimate Vocabulary

R/

[Reformation of Equality – Christ's formed doctrine]
rehearsed(for) – might be fair
  rehearsed(against) – might be unfair
religion(sectarianism) – forbidden
    Mark 9:38
renounce – to give up something bad; repent / requirement
repentance(repent) – a change of mind
reproach – blame falsely
  slander –
requirements1 – conditions of Bible/God
  restrictions1 –
  forbidden1 –
restoration2 – Jesus restores
resurrection – prophecy
  reincarnation – false prophecy
righteous – requirement
  self-righteous – forbidden
  unrighteous – forbidden
righteous requirement of the L/law – Matt. 22:37, 39

  remission of sins – repentance
    Acts 2:38
ring around the collar – "Irish Spring"
"Round-Up" – carcinogen"
  weed killer –

Composite Shēvā/Shēwā (ְ) Vowels			
pat	ă	ֲ	14
set	ĕ	ֱ	15
hot	ŏ	ֳ	16
Combination Vowels			
fine	ī	י ִ	17
have	ăv	ו ַ	18
have	ăv	יו ַ	19
hay	ay	י ֵ	20
[dialect]	āv to av	יו ָ	21
	ī	י ָ	22
	yi	י ְ	23
	ī	י ֶ	24

Legitimate Vocabulary

S/

   sabotage – add or take away from Bible forbidden

   sacrifice(altar) – atonement / thanksgiving, praise, & works

   sacrilegious – against the divine

   salvation(saved) –

   saturated fat – LDL
     unsaturated fat – HDL

   scholar – [trained writer]
     Scribes –

   sealant; urethane… –

   seclusion – requirement
     isolation – forbidden

   secular – worldly vocabulary
     nonsecular – Bible vocabulary

   [seebock effect] – elec. from heat

   seeding the air – homemade snow or rain by chemical reaction

   semi-colon – ;

   Semper Fi – Always Faithful

   serene composure – no demons

   shaken –

   shaman(shamanism) – "Satanism"
     medicine man – satanic witchcraft

   shortcomings –
     midlife crisis –

   short-hand – writing w/o vowels

	ee	יִ	25
	?	וּ	26
	āv	וָ	27
	chā	ךָ	28[?]
choking sound	chth	ךְ	29[?]

Legitimate Vocabulary

S/
- shortnessof breath – OTC(ABO) or med oxy.
- "silent partner" – [unChristian]
- singular –
  - plural –
- sleep – requirement
  - "deep sleep – forbidden"

Prayer

Blank for family pictures
for visual prayers.

Legitimate Vocabulary

S/

   smudging – purification by smoke
                (Catholics do it too)
   snake attractant gel –
   soluable; water… –
     fat soluble –
   sovereign – most high
   stale beer2 – "metaphor for stale words"
   stand – steadfast requirement
   stare"; "If they stare let them… –
   steadfast(firm) – not stubborn but firm
   stopping point –
     "mile marker" –
   strictness – is forbidden Col. 2:20
   "summit" – 'meeting of countries'
   superficial – fake
   supernatural – the unexplainable
   survival; #1 rule for… – not to panic; but
                    not always
   syllable – pauses between letters of words
   synchronicity – an omen; not always bad
   syntax – [formation of a sentence and or
          organizing of a sentence]

Prayer

Blank for family pictures
for visual prayers.

Legitimate Vocabulary

T/
- tabernacle – Moses Church
  - ark – ark holds the 10 Commandments
  - synagogue – Jew Church
- take heed – pay attention
- "take it one day at a time" –
- temple – flesh & bones w/ HS(Church1)
- text – a work of doctrine
- thanksgiving2 – giving thanks(victory/gate)
- The book of John – 'the book of Eternal Life'
- The book of Revelation(Reveal) –
- "The Faith Chapter" – Heb. 11
- "The Golden Rule" – Matt. 7:12
- ["The good outweighs the bad"] – deciding a medicine
- "The Morning Star" – Jesus
- time & Eternal – 2 places of time, & 1 place of Eternal (3 Heavens)
- tithe(tīthe) – 10% to Church, Jewish Cele., & or charity tithe
- tourniquet – wrap to slow blood loss
- transgressions – sins of known Laws; "stepping over" forbidden
  - sins – sins other than 'transgressional' sins

tribulation –
   oppression –
Trinity(Triune) – Father, Son, & HS
triune being – spirit, soul, & body of one
twelve legions of angels – 2nd coming "more than 12"
"Two wrongs don't make a right" –

Prayer

Blank for family pictures
for visual prayers.

Legitimate Vocabulary

U/
   uncharted territory – following Christ
                             God's will
   unexpected event – may provide opportune
   unlĕavĕn – bread w/o yeast

Prayer

Blank for family pictures
for visual prayers.

Legitimate Vocabulary

V/
  "verbal contract" –
    "written contract" –
  vision quest – 'an [indian] asceticism';
                 in search of an answer
                (others do it too)
    [smudging] – purification w/ smoke
                (Catholics do it too)
  vocabulary – list of words for meanings
    definitions – meanings

Prayer

Blank for family pictures
for visual prayers.

Legitimate Vocabulary

W/
   wait – requirements
     watch –
     stay awake – healthfully like
     pray –
   water-resistant – not immersed
     water-proof – immersible
   Word – is sword, but
     sword – is not Word
   "world" – worldly people are not
        Heavenly people
     World – is Heavenly people
   worry – forbidden Matt. 6:34
     frustration – same thing

Prayer

Blank for family pictures
for visual prayers.

Legitimate Vocabulary

X/

Prayer

Blank for family pictures
for visual prayers.

Legitimate Vocabulary

Y/

Prayer

Blank for family pictures
for visual prayers.

Legitimate Vocabulary

Z/
zealous – extreme circumstances require
   extreme measures requirement
overprotective –

'I'm happily Christian, not Catholic.'
A native of Powell, Wyoming, Arlen D.
Michaels washed dishes, maintenance,
mechanic, construction, roughneck,
electrical, carpentry, & entrepreneur.
He is the dad to Shane Michael.
In addition to writing and language,
Arlen D. Michaels enjoys praying,
personal and bible meditation, exōrcising &
exercising, helping people, hiking,
backpacking, sport fighting, & science.
Behold the Heart of My Mended Scars:
Revealing Poetic Insights by a Mystic
is his first published work.
'I lost count at 7 near-death experiences,
I was almost hit by a bullet,
I was in a coma,
Escaped life threatening diseases,
Been on a cane for two and a half years,
Survived almost being crippled from
cholesterol medicine,
Ate frozen food desperately,
Drank poison(alcohol),
Nearly drowned from my saliva,
Been lost and wet in darkness,
Persecuted from all directions,
Heart Attack, Scurvy, PTSD,
spit blood, peed blood, crapped blood,
Nearly died from old age at 42,
Outnumbered, Outflanked, Outdone,
I'm sure many had it worse;
Inspiration from Heb. 11:33-35
Survived by Faith, Bible, & Love'
Bible Understood:
Confess sins to God only with
thought only / 1 John 5:18
is his(this) second published work.

www.ingramcontent.com/pod-product-compliance
Lightning Source LLC
Chambersburg PA
CBHW060339170426
43202CB00014B/2825